WOLF: The Self-Absorbed Christian Marriage

By Marj Buchholz-Castronova, M.S.

For Amanda

I am SO proud of the woman you have chosen to be,
in spite of the obstacles you encountered

ACKNOWLEDGEMENTS

Where does one even begin to acknowledge all those who played a role in the development of a book? I would not even be the person I am without all of the contributions of others to my life. So, I would be remise to not acknowledge all those who impacted my life, even if your name isn't mentioned here. First, and foremost is God! I truly believe He crafted and continues to craft my life's story. Second, to my daughter Amanda, you are more precious to me than you can even imagine. In spite of my failings, you survived and are an amazing woman. Next is my husband Mike, you have shown me how it feels to be really loved and cherished. You are my best friend! And, you have enriched my life with your family! I was blessed with three extra daughters, Lezlie, Lauren, and Anna, and more son-in-laws and grandchildren than I ever imagined. I owe a debt of gratitude to my brother, Greg, who indeed is also a dear friend. Your wisdom and belief in me has always been a source of encouragement in life. Seriously, how cool is it that my brother is one of my closest friends. As time goes, I realize more and more the amazing sacrifices my parents made to raise me. Your love has given me a strong foundation to build from. I blessed with the most amazing circle of friends. They have over the years put up with hours and hours of listening to me as I processed what was going on in my life: Diane, Sandy, Kim, Debbie, Irene & Rick, Sherri & Jim, DeeDee, Tina, Teddy & Pam, Bill, Mark, Steve, Natalie, Amy & Jon, Mary, Joe & Letty, and Ann. Each of you played a key role in my journey. Thank you to the professionals in my life who were wise mentors and friends: Dr. Mark O'Dell, Dr. John Grogan, and Dr. Toni Zimmerman. I have learned from the best! And, I would even be remise to not be grateful for those situations and persons that were harmful as God has and is using them for His good.

The contributions to the actually writing of this book are endless. Every step of this book was covered by a Writing Prayer Team: Sandy, Sherri, Debbie, Kim, Jayne, Irene, Greg, Amanda, and Merlelynn. Thank you for lifting this project up before the Lord. As I moved toward working through the challenges of publishing, this team expanded to include many more...including people I don't know. There are also the cheerleaders of my writing, your words meant more to me than you realize. I also owe a debt of gratitude to those who edited, and edited, and edited. An extra special thanks to Amanda, Sandy P., and Greg for your grammer, spell checks, and sentence restructuring. And, to you mom for catching the biggest error of all! Special thanks to Merlelynn, Adrian, Steve C., Natalie, Joan, Steve T., Bart, and Dave for getting me gate passes to publishers. And then there is Marc Andrew Stephens (www.maswork.com)...you created a cover that rocks and I am lucky you are my friend! I am sure I have missed someone in my acknowledgements and I request your grace. My lack of memory in no way should minimize your contribution. My clients stories have been adjusted to protect confidentiality, but the integrity of each of their stories remains intact. It was a was a privilege and honor to journey with you in your stories and thank you for your willingness to share your stories so others could be encouraged and find hope!!!!!

Marj Buchholz-Castronova, M.S.

WOLF: The Self-Absorbed Christian Marriage

TABLE OF CONTENTS

Introduction: Is this book for you?

I wonder if you picked up this book because you are completely disillusioned with your Christian marriage. Maybe you already have a library full of self-help books on how to have a successful marriage, but despite your best efforts, things are still bad. I wonder if good intentioned friends have given you marital advice, but it has felt more like a visit from one of Jobs "comforters". I also wonder if your friends think that your spouse is wonderful and that you are a little off balance. They see one person in public and you see someone completely different at home. If you can relate to these thoughts, you my friend may be married to a wolf in sheep's clothing.

My heart goes out to you. I have personally been there. I have journeyed with hundreds of spouses who have been there. There is hope. Except, hope isn't what you think it is. Hope doesn't mean you will live happily ever after. Hope doesn't mean your spouse will get it. Hope doesn't mean that you won't get a divorce. Hope doesn't have any absolutes. As Hebrews 12 advises, there are many saints who have gone before us and died without their hopes being fulfilled. My dear friend, hope starts with you. It has nothing to do with whether your spouse gets it or steps up to the plate. It has to do with you becoming the spouse that God designed you to be! You have a choice. You can continue to try to be the spouse your partner tells you to be. Or, you can just stop trying and do what you want to do. Or, you can learn to be the kind of spouse that God wants you to be. The choice is yours. I believe that becoming the kind of spouse God wants you to be is the choice with the most mercy. It is the choice which best fits who God created you to be.

I am also assuming that if you were drawn to this book, you may indeed be married to what I refer to as a self-absorbed Wolf. The typical marital sermons and marriage relationship books aren't going to do the trick. The advice and skills offered in those books and sermons are usually sound, but they are often based on the assumption that two people are working together on their marriage. You can't have an "I feel _______, when you do _________", conversation with a self-absorbed Wolf. He or she will eat your words! You can't have fair negotiations with a self-absorbed Wolf, simply because they don't negotiate.

If your marriage has left you feeling confused, anxious, crazy, or lonely, you may be married to a self-absorbed Wolf. If you are starting to doubt yourself and your perspective on what is happening, you may be married to a self-absorbed Wolf. If you feel trapped in your marital vows, you may be married to a self-absorbed Wolf.

I am inviting you to go on a journey with me. Trails have been blazed by those who have gone before you. I know it is hard for you to still trust and believe that there may actually be a way out of your pain, but there is. God promises that He works all things together for good (Romans 8:28). He has done it for me. He has done it for the clients I have worked with. And, He can do it for you.

Chapter I
There Are Wolves Amongst You!

Beware of false teachers who come disguised as harmless sheep, but are wolves and will tear you apart.
Matthew 7:15 LB

Once upon a time there was a good little girl who tried to follow all the rules and do all the right things. She went to church and did her memory work. She went to school and did her homework. The good little girl even went to the right Christian college and married the right Christian boy. She thought if she did all the right things, then the right things would happen to her. She thought she would live happily ever after.

But, what the good little girl never did was learn to listen to her own voice.

The good little girl grew up to be a good Christian woman. In her marriage, she tried to follow all the rules and do all the right things. She went to church and read Christian marriage books. The books told her the right rules, including sacrifice and submission. Her marriage may have looked like the perfect Christian marriage, but inside she was sad and very lonely. Inside her voice started to speak, but it was a very negative voice and it pointed out what she didn't have. It pointed out that the man she married didn't follow the rule of loving her like Christ loved the church. The voice pointed out what he wasn't doing. It pointed out all she was doing. It pointed out that no matter what she did, it wasn't enough. The voice scared the good Christian woman. The voice didn't match the rules. It matched what she was experiencing. The good Christian woman wasn't living happily ever after…

But, the good Christian woman had started listening to her voice even though it scared her.

The good Christian woman was now in a bind. The rules weren't working. Doing the right thing wasn't working. No matter what she tried, her marriage wasn't working. She thought about divorce, but it didn't follow rules. She wondered how God could let this happen to her. None of it made sense. How could you do what you were suppose to do and not have it work? Meanwhile, the good Christian woman was learning to listen to her voice in parenting and it was working. She was learning to listen to her voice at work and it was working. She was learning to listen to her voice in other relationships and it was working. In all these other roles, she was learning it wasn't about living happily ever after...

But, the good Christian woman's voice still wasn't happy with her marriage.

There were still no options available to her in her marriage. She knew it was important to do the right thing, but her motives for doing the right thing were changing. She was learning the gift of giving without receiving. Then one night, after she had been backed into yet another corner in her marriage, she heard a voice clearly say, "You can depend on me to meet ALL your needs, including the ones in your marriage". The voice also told her to stop focusing on what her husband was or wasn't doing. She knew it was HIS voice. The more she rested in HIM to meet her needs, the more she started to hear HIS voice. HE started leading her to do things in her marriage for the sake of serving HIM, not because another did or didn't deserve something. She was learning that living happily ever after had something to do with giving to others, not getting from others...

By entering the scariness of her own voice, she had discovered HIS voice.

She realized that HE had been there the whole way. HE had been guiding her path. She realized that having a good marriage had become an idol and it had been more important than HE had been. She realized that HE had created her and He wanted her to know who HE had created her to be. It was in knowing herself that she began to understand what it meant to be transformed into Christ's image. If she didn't have her own reflection, she wouldn't be able to see where He was transforming her. As she started embracing her own voice, she was able to surrender it to HIM. The good Christian woman's once upon a time, fairy tale story, had become a real story, a transforming story.

Did you follow all the rules? Did you marry a Christian? Did you assume that in marrying a Christian, you would be blessed with a good marriage? Are you surprised at how difficult marriage is? Is your spouse self-absorbed? Are you self-absorbed? Every Christian needs to do a daily heart check. Marriage is one of the easiest places for our self-absorption to be exposed. If you did things your way in your marriage today, your self-absorption needs to be checked. Or maybe, you did things your spouse's way. Guess what? You may still need to do a heart check based on the motivation of your yes. Sometimes our yes's are motivated by fears of not wanting to take a stand. Remember Jonah? He got swallowed by a whale because he didn't want to take a stand against the people of Nineveh. He was doing what he wanted rather than what God had asked him to do. He was motivated by his selfishness.

There is a risk in starting to deal with your own self-absorption; it will start exposing the character of your spouse. As God transforms you into the kind of spouse He desires you to be, and you stop reacting to your spouse's behaviors, his or her character will be revealed. This will give your spouse the opportunity to see his or her own selfish reactions. Beware! If you are married to a self-absorbed Wolf, you aren't dealing with a naive sheep. Wolves have a different nature and they won't easily let themselves be exposed.

I remember sitting and listening to Mary tell me her story. It was one of those shocking Wolf stories. As her story unfolded, it was evident her life was being shattered by a destructive person, who at best was emotionally disconnected and completely self-absorbed, and at worst, a possible Narcissist. As a marriage and family therapist, I know there are two sides to the story, but in this case, the evidence was stacked against the spouse. Her husband, who was known as a godly man, was leaving his wife and family for another woman. I wondered if he was thinking about the effect his actions would have on others: the men who served with him, the men who served under him, the men he mentored, or the couples he and his wife mentored. What about Mary? She thought she had a secure and committed marriage even though it had been difficult at times. What about his two teenage children? How would it affect their view of a Christian father, a Christian marriage, and a Christian husband? What about the body of believers who had experienced what appeared to be a healthy Christian couple for years?

Of course, we all have heard stories like this. Sometimes it is the husband who leaves for another partner. Sometimes it is the wife. Certainly sin tightened its grip on this person. Sin always includes self-absorption when a person is seeking what is best for himself or herself regardless of the cost to others. Yet, in Mary's story, I heard more than the typical story of an affair. Underneath her story, I heard the undertones of possible Wolf lurking—a Wolf who was dressed in sheep's clothing. During countless sessions with clients over the years and from my own personal experiences, I have developed a list of symptoms that diagnoses a lurking Wolf. In Mary's story, I want to show you how the Wolf was exposing himself.

There was a long-term web of deception.

He had dated the other woman in high school. He had an affair with the other woman early on in his marriage, but his spouse never knew. He had stayed in contact with the woman throughout the whole marriage. She was "just a friend". A Wolf is a master at deception, and the spouse is oftentimes filled with confusion over his or her own perception of reality.

There was manipulation.

There was a campaign to create a favorable impression of himself and an unfavorable one of his spouse in the church. No one knew about his history with the other woman; she was just an old friend he had recently bumped into. He had raised his children to side with him because their mom was an angry woman. A Wolf is a master at manipulation, and the spouse is often filled with unresolved anger that he or she can't understand.

He was charming.

People loved his engaging personality. He was fun. He appeared to be warm and caring. People were blind to the self-purpose in his actions; friends and acquaintances were mere pawns on his chess board. A Wolf is a master at charming people, and the spouse often feels alone and isolated in his or her world of pain at home because no one will believe them. In fact, the more the spouse tries to talk with others, the crazier he or she appears.

There was blame toward the other spouse.

His wife was verbally abusive. She was controlling. She was angry. Consequently, the finger was pointed at her faults rather than owning up to his long-term affair and deception over the years. It always takes two to dance in a marriage. For every unhealthy action in a marriage, there is always a choice of reacting in a healthy or unhealthy way. We all have the wolf-like tendency to blame the other person, but a

Wolf will never take responsibility unless it serves his or her purpose. Oftentimes, the spouse becomes culpable in an attempt to try and resolve the problems.

There was an unwillingness to see reality.

He had rationalized his affair as God bringing this person into his life. He ignored the sexual infidelity; rules were beyond him when it served his purpose. He hid behind the facade of the "life-time friend". He only saw his perspective and was blind to his sin. A Wolf only sees one way—his way! If a wolf sees another perspective, it is because it serves his or her purpose in some way. The spouse is left feeling confused and has a hard time sorting through what is really going on. Sadly, in marriages involving wolves, therapists are even ill equipped to recognize what is going on. They just know they are stuck and can't figure out what is true and what isn't.

"Vengeance is mine," says the Wolf.

A few Christians had the courage to confront him. He hastily deemed them unsympathetic and unsupportive of his horrible marriage, after which cutting them off entirely. When a Wolf's true heart is exposed, he or she can become vengeful in order to salvage and protect his or her image. A Wolf will stop at nothing. A Wolf relentlessly twists the truth, spreads rumors, and stirs up trouble, all in order to get the spotlight off of himself or herself.

Wolves lack empathy and are blind to other's needs.

He disregarded the effect his affair would have on his wife. In his mind, she had brought this on herself through her behavior as a wife. He never considered how the affair would affect his children; he had sacrificed too many years of his life with this angry woman. He never considered the effect his actions had on those he had mentored in the church; they were supposed to be looking to God, not him, and if they knew all the sacrifices he had made, they would understand. It was all about him, what he had done, and what he had been through.

He didn't think about all the confusion his actions would have on the lives he influenced as they wrestled with finding truth while lacking facts. A Wolf is out to take care of himself or herself and is not concerned with the welfare of others. If a Wolf gives the appearance of care and concern, it is only to benefit him or herself.

One plus one doesn't equal two in Wolf Math.

The wife thought she had a solid, committed marriage. Yet, her spouse had been having an ongoing affair throughout the couple's whole marriage. The church thought they had a great marriage as they mentored young couples. If the couple had such a great marriage, how did the children believe that their mom was an angry, controlling person and their dad was their protector? Reality is never what it appears to be in a home where there is a Wolf. Wolves are masters at disguises and telling stories! A Wolf will use whatever resources he or she has to get what he or she wants, including using the appearance of faith and the misuse and abuse of scripture to get his or her way!

As the web was unraveled, the truth was revealed, and a wolf in sheep's clothing was unmasked!

I can not tell you how many times I have heard this story! I expect to hear this story from nonbelievers—they lack the motive for the love that believers possess, and they do not trust in God to meet their needs. They rely entirely on themselves to meet their needs. Unfortunately, this is the story I also hear in countless Christian marriages. We are called to love! We are called to sacrificial love! We are called to unconditional love! 1 Corinthians 13 doesn't leave room for my way; however, national statistics for divorce rates have long been equivalent between nonbelievers and Christians. Sadly, it was recently reported that the Christian divorce rate exceeded that of the secular. We, as believers, are obviously doing something wrong. In my close group of Christian girlfriends, four of us got married right out of college and within one year, two of those marriage had ended in divorce. Twelve years later, my own marriage ended in divorce. Somehow, even though we were all committed Christ-followers and firm believers in the covenant of marriage, only one of us—25% of our group—remains married today. Why? I believe the biggest obstacle in a marriage is yourSELF. Self-absorption is the single most destructive weapon of the enemy!

In this "what's in it for me" society, self-absorption has become the norm. Even acts of generosity and kindness are used as means of attaining recognition and awards, rather than quiet self-sacrifice as Jesus calls us to in Matthew 6:1-4. We are like the Pharisees who fasted in public (Matthew 6:16-18), so others will know how holy we are. When a marriage suffers from self-absorption it is filled with confusion, unmet needs, and questions. For the Christian person committed to his or her covenant marriage, this is especially painful as he or she begins to feel trapped in his or her vows. Faith and commitment becomes questionable as he or she wrestles to find answers

1. *Did I really hear God when I felt Him leading me to marry this person?*

2. *I don't understand, I did everything God's way before I got married. I stayed pure, I followed all the rules yet my marriage isn't what a Christian marriage is supposed to be.*

3. *I don't believe in divorce, but I am miserable. I have so many emotional needs that are unmet. I feel empty inside.*

4. *I am so confused, my Christian friends keep telling me I just need to be submissive, but my husband never considers my feelings or needs.*

5. I am so confused, my Christian friends keep telling me I just need to serve my wife more, but she never considers my feelings or needs. I am so alone.

6. I thought I married this strong Christian person, and here I am several years into the marriage, and my spouse doesn't want anything to do with God.

There are no easy answers or solutions to these painful questions and thoughts; however, if you find you relate to them, this book can shed light on your situation. From my own personal experiences and the countless cases I have worked with in therapy, I am convinced that a marriage built on self-absorption is one of the most painful situations to endure. I am also convinced that when you are married to a Wolf, the standard Christian marriage books and teachings only add more pain, confusion, and questions. I believe the rules change when you are married to a Wolf. Additional scriptures and teachings are necessary for survival!

In Matthew 7:15 LB, Jesus says, *"Beware of false teachers who come disguised as harmless sheep, but are wolves and will tear you apart."* The Message translation puts it *"Be wary of false preachers who smile a lot, dripping with practiced sincerity. Chances are they are out to rip you off some way or other."*

If there are false teachers, have you ever considered what life must be like for their spouses? And, don't forget the Pharisees and Sadducees had spouses too. Can you image what their home lives were like? Jesus warned us in Matthew 16:6 LB, *"Watch Out!" Jesus warned them; "beware of the yeast of the Pharisees and Sadducees."* Have you ever thought about the yeast in their homes?

If you are married to a Wolf, I am pretty sure you are self-sacrificing to a fault. You are more than willing to look at yourself. You have prayed, sought wise counsel, have a library full of books on how to improve your marriage, but to no avail.

No matter what you do, no matter what responses or actions you have changed, nothing in the marriage seems to change. You are feeling hopeless and at the end of your rope. You may have even tried marriage counseling, but it didn't work. And, now you are trapped.

There is still hope, I promise. Even better, God promises!

Romans 8:24 still holds true, "*We are saved by trusting. And trusting means looking forward to getting something we don't yet have – for a man who already has something doesn't need to hope and trust that he will get something.*" God has also given you strategies in His word to deal with wolves. Matthew
10:16 MSG says, "*Stay alert. This is hazardous work I'm assigning you. You're going to be like sheep running through a wolf pack, so don't call attention to yourselves. Be as cunning as a snake, inoffensive as a dove.*"

Our childhood tales even told us and warned us about the nature of wolves. Little Red Riding Hood[1] trusted the Wolf because he was "dripping with practiced sincerity", and she naively gave him directions to her Grandmother's house, only to discover later that he had eaten her Grandmother. Thank goodness, Little Red Riding Hood learned from her first encounter with the Wolf how to be "cunning as a snake and inoffensive as a dove".

Likewise, The Three Little Pigs[2] encounter the trickery of a Wolf. I'm sure you remember the tale…frustrated by a lack of sugar and the unwillingness of his neighboring pigs to help him, the wolf resorts to blowing down the pigs' houses. While the first two pigs were distracted and mindless, the third pig was as "cunning as a snake" and overcame the wolf.

Did you know the Wolf discloses his own version of the story in *The True Story of the Three Little Pigs!* by Jon Scieszka[3]. The wolf turns the story around and claims that he was falsely accused and misunderstood. He was simply making a birthday cake for his sweet, elderly granny and ran out of sugar. When he innocently went to borrow a cup from his straw house dwelling neighbor, his allergies caused him to sneeze, and the house blew down, inevitably killing the pig. So, there was this great ham dinner just lying there in the straw. No one could have resisted. You can only imagine the rest of the story with all it's twisting of the truth, rationalizing, and blaming. There are Wolves in the world, there are Wolves in the church, and there are Wolves in Christian marriages. We as a church need to stop being so naive! We need to wake up and smell the Wolf breath!!!

Jesus encountered Wolves throughout His time on earth. He survived King Herod, outwitted the Pharisees and Sadducees, resisted Satan's temptations, and even recognized the wolf-like tendencies of Judas. Jesus rested in His Father's sovereignty! He sought wisdom from His Father! And He stayed true to who He was, amidst the selfish sinning around Him. He was without sin!

One needs to look no further than an encounter between Jesus and the Pharisees to discover how He dealt with the Wolves around Him. Recall Matthew 12: 22-24 MSG, *"Next a poor demon-afflicted wretch, both blind and deaf, was set down before him. Jesus healed him, gave him his sight and hearing. The people who saw it were impressed –"this has to be the Son of David!" But the Pharisees, when they heard the report, were cynical. "Black magic," they said. "Some devil tricks he's pulled from his sleeve."*

Step back for one minute. Think of this…Jesus has just healed a blind and deaf man, while the "godly people of the time" are accusing him acting on Satan's behalf. If you are in a self-absorbed marriage, I am sure you have been accused of evil, but before you surrender to this manipulation, listen to Jesus' response:

Jesus confronted their slander. "A judge who gives opposite verdicts on the same person cancels himself out; a family that's in a constant squabble disintegrates; if Satan banishes Satan, is there any Satan left? If you're slinging devil mud at me, calling me a devil kicking out devils, doesn't the same mud stick to your own exorcists? But if it's by God's power that I am sending the evil spirits packing, then God's kingdom is here for sure. How in the world do you think it's possible in broad daylight to enter the house of an awake, able-bodied man and walk off with his possessions unless you tie him up first? Tie him up, though, and you can clean him out. This is war and there is no neutral ground. If you're not on my side, you're the enemy; if you're not helping, you're making things worse." Matthew 10: 25-30 MSG

When you are married to a self-absorbed Wolf, you, my dear friend, have been tied up and who God created you to be has been stripped away by your Wolf's insatiable appetite! It is your responsibility to be who God called you to be, in spite of the obstacles before you. If you continue to allow yourself to be fettered by the Wolf, you are helping the Enemy in his battle. Remember, Jesus didn't leave us empty handed in our battle. In Matthew 10, Jesus is sending His disciples out with their marching orders and He is very clear in his warning of wolves and how to interact with them.

Give me a few more moments of your time before you conclude that I am some bitter, divorced Christian woman! We all have our own wolfish tendencies, and I certainly had and still have some of mine. Think about this… If we are at war, wouldn't it be an amazing strategy of the enemy to have Christians marry one another and then work to blind themselves to their selfishness. In Beth Moore's book, *When Godly People Do Ungodly Things[4]*, she writes, "Satan loves secrets and often works through disguises, masquerades, and shrouds. He wants things to stay in the dark because he knows the moment we expose it to the light of God, he's finished. Deception is an absolute in every stronghold, but the nature of seductive deception is that the lies are often well masked for a while. " The enemy knows the harder the heart, the more the person becomes like a wolf! The enemy also likes to twist truth, so why not twist leadership and submission to create confusion for spouses. Better yet, raise children in those "Christian" homes who will follow in their parent's footsteps.

What a mess!

I also believe that you didn't intentionally marry a wolf. Sheep don't run out looking for a wolf to hook-up with. Remember, wolves "smile a lot" and are "dripping with practiced sincerity". Wolves present themselves as sheep when you meet them. But Wolves are out to "tear you apart". In *The Screwtape Letters[5]*, C.S. Lewis exposes the enemy's strategies though a series of letters from Satan to his demons on how to destroy and trick believers. In one of Uncle Screwtape's (Satan's) letters to Wormwood (his demon), he says, "*You must bring him to a condition in which he can practice self-examination for an hour without discovering any of those facts about himself which are perfectly clear to anyone who has ever lived in the same house with him or worked in the same office.*" Think about the strategy of having a strongly devoted follower of Christ who is a "harmless sheep" meet a wolf who comes "dripping with practiced sincerity". Can you imagine the kind of marriage they would have? If you are reading this book, my guess is that you can.

In either case, whether you have been acting like a Wolf or have been deceived by a real Wolf in sheep's clothing, Jesus continues to give direction..."*There's nothing done or said that can't be forgiven. But if you deliberately persist in your slanders against God's Spirit, you are repudiating the very One who forgives. If you reject the Son of Man out of some misunderstanding, the Holy Spirit can forgive you, but when you reject the Holy Spirit, you're sawing off the branch on which you're sitting, severing by your own perversity all connection with the One who forgives. If you grow a healthy tree, you'll pick healthy fruit. If you grow a diseased tree, you'll pick worm-eaten fruit. The fruit tells you about the tree!*" (Matthew 12:31-33 MSG)

Here is my challenge: despite your pain and confusion, I am going to ask you to stop focusing on your spouse's fruit or lack of it! I am going to ask you repeatedly to surrender to your loving Father in Heaven and bear good fruit, regardless of the marriage you are in. God knows your spouse and his or her heart better than you do.

God knows what is going on. Matthew 12:34 MSB says, *"You have minds like a snake pit! How do you suppose what you say is worth anything when you are so foul-minded? It's your heart, not the dictionary that gives meaning to your words."* Listen to those words again…

It is your heart, not the dictionary that gives meaning to your words!

God knows your heart! God knows your spouse's heart! My dear, hurting friend, let God deal with your spouse's heart and surrender your heart to God so it matches your words and actions! But, beware! When your spouse gives you "flowery dictionary words," and his or her actions aren't congruent with those words, you are encountering self absorption and possibly a Wolf. If this is the case, you will need some new tactics.

Jesus also says, *"A good person produces good deeds and words season after season. An evil person is a blight on the orchard. Let me tell you something: Every one of these careless words is going to come back to haunt you. There will be a time of reckoning. Words are powerful; take them seriously. Words can be your salvation. Words can also be your damnation."* (Matthew 12:35-37 MSG) When you respond to your spouse's self-absorbed words with your own self-absorption, even when it is a reaction to his or her painful words, your words will come back to haunt you. When you respond to your spouse's self-absorbed words with wisdom and discernment, your words will be your saving grace! It is so important to beware and be wise when for dealing with a self-absorbed Wolf.

There is no safer thing for you to do than surrender to your Father. You may wrestle with Him as He transforms you into His image. You may be frustrated that your spouse appears to be getting off the hook. You may be disappointed in your limited view of what God is up too. You will feel like God's timing is off. But, rest assured…there is no safer place.

Proverbs 3:26 MSG promises *"Because God will be right there with you; He'll keep you safe and sound."*

Chapter II
He's the wolf. No, She's the wolf.

Humans have an almost limitless capacity for self-deception.
John Ortberg

We must remain open to seeing the facts from a new perspective and equally open to the possibility that our perception is distorted by the log in our own eye.
Dan B. Allender & Temper Longman, III

Let's start with a test…read the following passage from 1Corinthians 13:4-7 MSG.

Love never gives up.
Love cares more for others than for self.
Love doesn't want what it doesn't have.
Love doesn't strut,
Doesn't have a swelled head,
Doesn't force itself on others,
Isn't always "me first,"
Doesn't fly off the handle,
Doesn't keep score of the sins of others,
Doesn't revel when others grovel,
Takes pleasure in the flowering of truth,
Puts up with anything,
Trusts God always,
Always looks for the best,
Never looks back,
But keeps going to the end.

Now be honest. When you were reading those verses, what are you thinking? Perhaps you thinking, "*I haven't learned to love like that,*" or maybe you were thinking "*My spouse doesn't love me like that.*" My guess is that most of you were thinking the latter, which means you have some work to do. Indeed, you may in fact be married to a self-absorbed Wolf, but all of us have some of our own self-absorption to deal with first. The truth is, if you don't deal with your own issues of self-absorption, you are on your own slippery slope to Wolfdom.

I understand that your pain is deep. I understand that your disappointment is vast. I understand that your emotional needs bank is empty. I understand that you feel your spouse doesn't meet any needs. The more empty our marriage bank, the more self-consumed we can become. Jesus gets it. After He had been fasting in the desert for forty days, I am sure He was starving. Did He eat when food was offered to him? Or, did he still focus on what His Father was calling Him to do? Even at His emptiest moments, He still followed His Father's will, rather than His perceived unmet needs. He knew His father and He trusted in His provision and His way. Philippians 4:7 MSG says, *"Don't fret or worry. Instead of worrying, pray. Let your petitions and praises shape your worries into prayers, letting God know your concerns. Before you know it, a sense of God's wholeness, everything coming together for good, will come and settle you down. It is wonderful what happens when Christ displaces worry at the center of your life."*

The thing is, when we get married, we start looking to our spouse to meet our needs. Certainly in the world this makes sense; in God's however, it doesn't. Christian marriages too often adopt the world's principles and forget that we are to have "no other gods, only the one true God," and if we are looking to our marriage or spouse to meet our needs, we have replaced God. Ultimately God, and only God, is who we are to look to. The primary purpose of your marriage isn't to meet your needs. Let me say that again, the primary purpose of your marriage isn't to meet your needs! It is to have a living example of Christ's relationship with the church! Marriage is a vehicle that God uses to transform us into Christ's image! A difficult marriage is the vehicle that God is using to transform you. If we are abiding in Christ and growing in our faith, ALL of us will encounter a vehicle that will teach us what it means to suffer with Christ.

Don't misunderstand me, God did design marriage to be a primary source of fulfillment. However, it is only one of the avenues He uses to meet your needs. So, when needs aren't being met in your marriage (for whatever reason), make your requests to God and stop being upset at your spouse. Your unmet needs reveal issues in your spiritual life. Where does your security lie? Is it in God, or is it really in your marriage, or your finances, or your friends, or your parents? Do you trust God? Do you want God to do things your way or His way? So often, the ideal of a godly marriage becomes an idol in and of itself.

There are a lot of things that contribute to our unmet needs and self-absorption. I think of it as a gradual, yet steady process with many rivers that flow into one source and ultimately can flood relationships and create massive damage. There are several rivers that have a major impact on our capacity to identify our emotional needs or to be able to meet the needs of others.

Our human needs:

One river is being human. God designed us with needs. When we don't have faith, the only way to get our needs met is to look toward other things. Once we have faith, we are supposed to depend on God to meet our needs, but taking care of our own needs, in our own way, is a hard habit to break. The Rev. Grimstead, one of my college professors, would always say, "The old man is a good swimmer, we need to drown him daily." Marriage often covertly becomes a way for us to legitimately try to meet our needs. In the process of trying to pick a good mate, we start generating a list of needs that we want met through marriage. (see Figure 1)

INDIVIDUAL

Future wife list:

1. **Godly wife**
2. **Sexual Fulfillment**
3. **Take care of home**
4.
5.

Figure 1

This is actually a wise thing to do. Neil Clark Warner, in his book *Date or Soul Mate: How to Know if Someone is Worth Pursuing in Two Dates or Less[6]* suggests you come up with a list of the ten things you want in a spouse and ten things you don't want in a spouse. We all have lists, even if we haven't written them down, that guide our way to Mr. or Mrs. Right. One day we meet someone who meets most of our list and we fall in love. This person is so good at meeting our needs. They want to spend time with us. They appear to be a living testament of what a godly man or godly woman is. They appear to have an amazing relationship with God. So, you decide they are the one and get married.

When you are falling love, it is SO easy to meet the other person's needs because you are thinking of them constantly. Somewhere after the "I Do," you get off track. Your prayerful list, even when based on scripture, becomes a Pharisee list. You begin to take the "law" and use it as a "set of rules and standards" (Matthew 23:1-4) to control your spouse and get your needs met how you want and when you want them. The law was always intended to be a mirror that reflected our heart and its alignment with God, not as a way to get someone else to meet our needs.

Our prayerful list of needs and desires become expectations. We then start playing the "should game," and with it, comes a lot of expectations. There are expectations of what a Christian marriage looks like and what a godly spouse looks like. There are expectations of what a submissive wife looks like. There are expectations of what a spiritual leader looks like as a husband. There are expectations of how a spouse should behave sexually. The expectations are endless (see Figure 2).

GOD

WIFE ________________________ **HUSBAND**

Expectations:

1. **Godly Spouse**
2. **Sexual Fulfillment**
3. **Emotional Fulfillment**
4. **Financial Security**

Figure 2

Our list isn't the problem. God has given us our desires and needs, but when they turn into expectations, we start having problems. Our expectations of others become our "self-absorption" as we attempt to fulfill our needs in the ways that we think they should be met. Our expectations of God being the provider are replaced by this expectation for our spouse. Our expectations take the focus off of what we are to do with 1 Corinthians 13. It becomes a list of what our partner should be doing, and we take on the role of pointing out his or her failings and sins against us.

In my case, I went from my parents supporting me financially to marrying right out of college and moving to where my husband got his first job, rather than going on to graduate school like I felt God was calling me to do. I have felt called to be a counselor since junior high. When I chose to sacrifice graduate school, I postponed God's calling on my life. I was prodded by my insecurity to get married, and underneath this came several expectations I began to place on my spouse. One of them was to be acknowledged for the "great sacrifice" I made in giving up graduate school. My "great sacrifice" may have appeared to be a selfless act to serve my husband; however, it came with strings: it wanted what it didn't have, it kept score, it didn't trust God, it didn't look for the best in its spouse, and it keep looking back. It was self-absorbed.

Our childhood experiences:

A second river is our childhood experiences. They impact the kind of spouse we choose, how we interact with our spouse, and how we react to our spouse. Some of you have had horrible experiences during childhood, which have left you feeling like you are broken beyond repair. Some of you grew up in what appeared to be a good home, but you keep finding yourself in dysfunctional relationships with dysfunctional people.

In childhood, we have legitimate needs. Our parents are God's designed way of meeting those needs. Your parents may have met basic needs (like food and shelter), but emotional needs weren't even considered. Biologically, for a child's right side of his or her brain to fully develop, the meeting of emotional needs is essential.

Our childhood experiences begin to dictate the story of how we define ourselves. I spent a good chunk of my early adult years believing that "I was stupid." I had plenty of experiences that spoke to the contrary; I graduated from high school with honors, I was accepted into college and graduated Cum Laude with three majors; I got my master's degree with a 4.0 in all my classes except one. Even with all those experiences that said I wasn't stupid, I had two early experiences that told me otherwise. One time, in an attempt to follow-through on discipline, my dad put a dunce cap on my head. I would never have remembered this experience, had my college roommate not given me a Precious Moment's figurine with a dunce cap on it, when I missed being on the Dean's List for getting a C in golf (I never claimed to be athletic). When I opened her gift, I started to cry and had a vague memory of wearing a dunce cap. I knew my dad to be a caring and compassionate man, so this memory was incongruent for me. My dad later admitted this and apologized. His words of acknowledging and apologizing opened the door for my healing. However, another experience early in my life had also helped seal this truth for me. My birthday is in August, so my parents put me in school early, but I wasn't ready developmentally, so I was held back in first grade. Even though I was told I wasn't ready developmentally, I still had memories of going to the special education class with other kids who were known for not being smart, so I thought I must have been one of them.

We all have experiences that build false beliefs into our thought process. These false beliefs then impact the way that we try to get our needs met. They also affect the way we are able to meet other people's needs. Every time one of these false beliefs is triggered, we have a reaction process of protecting ourselves. It is in this defense mechanism that we lash back at someone. In marriage, our false beliefs are triggered frequently. We have an opportunity to let these events instigate the healing process, or we can protect our own wounds with defenses. When we defend our wounds, we end up damaging others.

Our teaching/interpretations:

Another river is the teachings and interpretations of scriptures that get filtered through our experiences. A belief I was taught as a child is that "Authority is always right." My parents were motivated by good intentions. They wanted me to respect authority. My dad was a state trooper who experienced the effects of people who defied authority. There were few things that stirred my dad up including a religious person or preacher breaking the law. My dad lived by Romans 13:1-6 where we are instructed to obey the laws of the land. He saw acts of speeding by pastors or known Christians as a sin. He took care of the accidents caused by speeding, where afterwards he had to knock on the doors of family members and tell them loved ones had died (and he knew that if speed hadn't been involved, there was a good chance that lives would have been spared). His intention in teaching me to respect authority was good, but I didn't learn how to stand up for myself because there was always authority dictating my actions. When I heard the church's teaching on wives being submissive, I heard "husbands are always right." Ironically my college roommate, who was raised by her mom and grandmother, heard the same teaching, but she didn't hear husbands are always right. She heard that husbands were to love their wives like Christ loved the church. She didn't believe that authority was always right. Bottom line: when we hear a teaching, it gets sifted and interpreted through our experiences.

Each of these tributaries: the childhood river, the experience river, the teaching/interpretation river, and other rivers like personality, birth order, culture, gender, etc., begin to form into the our personal mighty Mississippi. But, when the Mississippi floods....beware! It is through the merging of rivers that we generate what we need, desire, and expect. If we are looking to a person or thing to meet these needs, we are in trouble. Only God can truly meet our needs.

For instance, one of our most basic needs is security. We try to meet this need in many tangible ways. Some of us try to meet it through our jobs; others try to meet it through a solid financial portfolio; and others surround themselves by relationships. These all appear to be legitimate ways to satisfy our need for security. Others try to ignore the need or are unaware of it and choose tactics that numb the pain like food, spending, alcohol, drugs, or sex. We will use anything to avoid feeling that our security need isn't being met. The reality is NOTHING, except a relationship with the Lord can complete this need.

In Brennan Manning's *The Importance of Being Foolish: How to Think Like Jesus[7]*, Manning discusses our security need in the context of intimacy and shares a quote from Ken Keyes, Jr., "*When your consciousness is preoccupied with striving toward what you feel to be your security needs, you are more isolated from people than at any other level. And your energy will be at its lowest. When you are preoccupied with security, you are trapped in conflicting conditions in your relationships with others. You create "others" as objects to help you become more secure—or as objects to fight because they threaten your security. On the security level you cannot love others since this level creates great distances between you and other people."* (65 & 66)

During brief moments in life, we may have tried to embrace the truth of Philippians 4:19 LB "*And it is he who will supply all your needs from his riches in glory, because of what Christ Jesus has done for us*". In reality, we don't begin to grasp what ALL means until we have—those things that we hold dear to us.

I remember in the early 80's hearing the following expression "Jesus isn't all you need, until He is all you have". Something in that expression spoke such truth to me that I wrote it on the inside jacket of my Bible, including the time, place and who said it—July 7, 1984 at the "Sonshine Festival" in Willmar, Minnesota spoken by Steve Camp. I couldn't grasp what it really meant; I hadn't lost enough; I hadn't surrendered enough; I hadn't figured out who I was; I was still having too many concrete needs being met by my parents and my new boyfriend (who eventually became my first husband). I remember seeing a girl from high school at the festival. I bet she knew what that statement meant. I remember being so thankful that she had found Jesus. She experienced nothing short of emotional torture by kids in our class. Rumor had it her parents drank a lot. I am sure her home life was just as bad as her school life. She knew Jesus was all she had! I didn't, Jesus wasn't all I had yet. I still had my family; I still had friends; I still had a roof over my head. And, I had a boyfriend. I didn't understand yet that…

"Jesus isn't all you need, until He is all you have."

Slowly over the years, things were stripped away, but not enough. I was always able to figure out how to compensate and get my needs met another way. I always had a lot of friends; I had developed a strong professional reputation; I now had a daughter; I still had my parents and brother, and I still had a husband, but I didn't feel like my needs were being met by my husband. I became attracted to another man. He seemed to meet my unmet emotional needs. However, my values system wouldn't let me act on my feelings. God protected me and moved our family to another state. My focus was still on trying to have a healthy marriage, one where people felt valued, respected, loved, and needs were met. I still didn't get it…

"Jesus isn't all you need, until He is all you have."

When I moved from one city to the other, I lost my professional self. I tried to recreate it, but that wasn't working. I had a bachelor's degree and in the new state you needed a master's degree or a technical brain to have value in the work force. So, I took my dream of going to graduate school for counseling off the back burner, which is what God had initially intended me to do. In the move, I also lost my church family and support system. I tried to find another church, but the church we had left was a forerunner in the seeker model and our new home didn't have one. I slowly built a support system, but those take time.

In graduate school, the dysfunction of my marriage became increasingly evident. I started seeing what some of the underlying issues were, but my focus was still on what my husband was and wasn't doing. In my eyes, he was the problem. I couldn't see how my way of getting needs met was part of the problem. I actually left my husband the fall of my second year, but the pain of not having my daughter with me all the time was too great and my belief in "death do us part, regardless" was too strong, so I went back. In doing so, I lost myself. I finally had lost something that made me start to see...

"Jesus isn't all you need, until He is all you have."

I knew full well going back into my marriage wasn't going to meet my needs. We saw the world differently. We were on different pages emotionally, financially, and spiritually. I saw my husband trying. For six months, we made a valiant effort and things appeared to be improving. We tried to reconcile the difficult areas. I am not going to go into details, as there are two perspectives and it wouldn't be fair to only tell you mine. My purpose is to share the lessons I learned from God's refining process and not about bashing my daughter's father. We both had shortcomings.

What I learned was that God was the person who provided for me financially, regardless of whether or not I had a spouse. I also started to realize that God could meet my emotional needs. It wasn't contingent on whether my husband was capable of this. We both related very differently in this area.

I started leaning on my relationship with God. I started learning who He was. A Kay Arthur study became a source of my understanding the names of God in a way I had never understood before. I started looking to God for practical and "impractical" financial provision. I started realizing God had an amazing sense of humor in the midst of all of it. A couple of stories stand out to me and are worth sharing.

I had an addiction to Peach Snapple and drinking it at $1.25 a bottle in the mid 1990's was an extravagance. When I found it on sale, I would buy a case. My husband and his family are very conservative financially, so as silly as it seems, Snapple was a source of contention. I remember one time, when my father-in-law was visiting, I brought home a case. I felt the need to defend my actions, "It was on sale." During that time, Snapple had a prize contest and ironically in that very case, I uncovered a winning cap earning me a free 27 inch Sony Trinitron television. I am not kidding you! The funnier part was that Sony delivered the television for free, to my front door, when I wasn't at home and my husband and in-laws were there. God was letting me know He provided extravagantly! I still watch that television today over 10 years later.

Another time, we had friends who called us and asked us to go to Hawaii with them for their 10th anniversary. It would be an all expense paid vacation staying at a five-star resort. All we had to do was come up with $1,000 of spending money. At the time, I was still in graduate school full-time, so I was completely unable to contribute financially. I had a small part-time job and the money I made went towards paying for my tuition and paying for some bills I had accrued during our separation. My husband and I were keeping our finances completely separate at the time as we were unable to find any negotiable space. My husband asked if we should go to Hawaii. For the first time, I truly let it be and trusted that if God wanted us to go, we would. The Marj of the past would have said. "Are you nuts? Of course we should go." Then I would have talked about charging it, about it being a once in a lifetime opportunity, about how neither of us had ever been to Hawaii, and about how this basically was a free trip. I told my husband I would leave that decision to him, as he was the person coming up with the $1,000 spending money. And I prayed. I surrendered. I said, "Lord it is yours. You know I would love to go to Hawaii, but you would need to make the way." I let it be. There was no fighting. There was no resentment or anger on my part. I was content to let God have His way. My husband decided not to go and that was his choice. He knew where he felt the money needed to go. He called the couple to tell them he wasn't going to go, but they weren't home. Then, about a week later, he told me that we were going to go. I knew God had changed his heart. I was excited, but in a different way. I was more in awe of God and His extravagant provision. The truth is...

"Jesus isn't all you need, until He's all you have"

When you depend on others, they will inevitably fail you in some way. They are human. We are human. Our individual needs are in constant collision with others. By nature, we are selfish and sinful. It is only when we embrace the one true source of life that we are able to realize He is the provider of all! Yes, He does sometimes provide through humans. But, He is the utmost provider. And when we understand this, we are able to learn to love like 1 Corinthians 13.

Philippians 4:19 LB says, *"And it is He who will supply ALL your needs from His riches in glory, because of what Christ Jesus has done for us."* In the verse prior, Paul says that God provided more than Paul needed. The couple who took us to Hawaii saw God as their provider, and they were passing His blessings onto us. God was providing above our need from His riches! God's riches also include the resources that don't appear to be directly linked to Him, like the Snapple Company.

Over and over again, God has provided abundantly. I have continuously received Starbuck's gift certificates when I couldn't afford my addiction: venti, decaf, nonfat, no foam lattes! I have been given a Louis Vuitton purse by a friend. When I was a single parent and struggling, dear friends gave me the money for my quarterly taxes. I bought a house in Las Vegas before the market soared and made over $200,000 which helped me survive my years as a single parent. God was the one who provided in all those cases, abundantly from His riches and glory because of what Christ Jesus did for me. I finally started to understand...

"Jesus isn't all you need, until He is all you have"

When I talk with a spouse in a difficult Christian marriage for the first time about this concept, it gives them hope. It also holds them highly accountable. From that moment forward, they are accountable to God for their interaction with their spouse, regardless of what their spouse is doing or isn't doing. We come back to that principle over and over and over.

I remember Cindy being pretty upset at what I was saying. She felt it let her husband Tim off the hook way too much because she believed he needed to step up to the plate. God had allowed her once sheltered world to come crashing in after they took in a fourth foster child who ended up having multiple special needs. Cindy and Tim had taken the child in because they believed God had led them to. Their once solid marriage started caving in under the strain of the special needs of the child. Up to that point, Cindy had been able to juggle her world with three adopted children, a business she ran and a successful marriage. The special needs of the fourth child were very taxing and she ended up selling her business in order to manage all the extra care and appointments that accompanied the child's care. People thought Cindy was crazy to create so much stress in her home life. God was moving her to understand that...

"Jesus isn't all you need, until He is all you have"

Tim did slowly step up to the plate. I have never seen two people so tenaciously cling to their covenant of marriage. They truly are living witnesses to me of what happens when people hold onto the covenant and the truth of marriage amidst the storm. They both learned to surrender, regardless of what the other's actions. They both clung to Jesus. When one wasn't surrendering, the other was. When one wasn't giving, the other was. They realized that there would be times when they were both depleted and there was nothing left. Over time, God restored their marriage. They both are learning what it means to cling to Jesus first and then live a life of 1

Corinthians 13.

Remember, your expectations in marriage put the focus on you and on what your spouse isn't doing, rather than on God's provision. I grew up in Minnesota, and I remember as a little child walking across the Mississippi, rock by rock, at the point where it is merely a little stream. I knew that in Minneapolis this was a huge river, and as it flowed south it got bigger and bigger, until it hit the Gulf of Mexico. But at its source, it was a small stream flowing out of Lake Itasca, a lake in northern Minnesota. Like a child, we need to go back to the one true, river source (see Figure 3).

GOD

MEETS MY NEEDS:
1. Security
2. Emotional Provision
3. Financial Provision
4. Sexual Fulfillment

WIFE **HUSBAND**

Question: Lord, What needs do you want me to meet in my spouse today to be the kind of spouse you called me to be?

Figure 3

We need to remember what is behind our expectations and our needs. We need to remember who meets ALL of our needs (Philippians 4:19). When we get married, the scripture verse doesn't change to...

And it is your spouse who will supply all your needs from his/her riches in glory, because of what Christ Jesus has done.

It doesn't even change to...

And it is your spouse who will supply 50% of all your needs from his/her riches glory, because of what Christ Jesus has done.

Think about this for a minute. When you have your eyes on your spouse to meet your needs, who are you angry or frustrated at? Your spouse, right? When you have your eyes on God to meet your needs (in His way, His time, from His riches), who are you angry and frustrated at? Maybe you are frustrated with yourself for not trusting Him more or maybe you are frustrated with God because His timing and His ways are different than yours.

Initially you may be mad at me. How dare I let your spouse off the hook with a question like that? Next, you may be mad at God, how dare He let your spouse off the hook for all the "shoulds". Just look at 1 Corinthians 13, look at what he or she should be doing. If you dig deeper and are honest, you will find that your anger or frustration is that you have taken your eyes off of Jesus as your source and put them on another human. Imagine what would happen in your marriage if you stopped looking to your spouse to be the provider of your needs and put your eyes back to God. Imagine all the pressure and expectations you would have taken off your spouse and your marriage.

Here is my challenge to you. Start taking the 1 Corinthians 13:4-7 test every day. In the morning, ask God to help you love your spouse, the way He wants you to. Next, ask God to meet your needs that day. In the evening, pray for God to help you see where you did love your spouse and where you still need to be transformed. Don't forget to thank God for meeting your needs during the day also!

Love never gives up.
Love cares more for others than for self.
Love doesn't want what it doesn't have.
Love doesn't strut,
Doesn't have a swelled head,
Doesn't force itself on others,
Isn't always "me first,"
Doesn't fly off the handle,
Doesn't keep score of the sins of others,
Doesn't revel when others grovel,
Takes pleasure in the flowering of truth,
Puts up with anything,
Trusts God always,
Always looks for the best,
Never looks back,
But keeps going to the end.

Chapter III
Wolves Come In Different Types of Sheep's Clothing

What keeps me feeling insecure are my addictive emotional needs, which must always be satisfied. When reality does not live up to my expectations, I become frustrated, angry, bitter, anxious, and resentful.
Brennan Manning

In her book *The Verbally Abusive Relationship[8]*, Patricia Evans describes a scientific experiment with frogs. If you put a frog in a pot of cold water, on a stove, and bring it to a slow boil, the frog will not jump out before the water boils, as it has adjusted to the slow temperature climb. If you put a frog into a pot of water that is already boiling, the frog will jump out.

Being in a relationship with a Wolf is comparable to this behavior. If you encounter a Wolf at his boiling point or when he doesn't have his sheep's clothing on, you would never enter a relationship with that person. However, if you encounter the Wolf when she is in her sheep's clothing, especially if you are at a vulnerable point in life, you will be deceived by her.

Genuine wolves usually prey upon the sick, weak, and old animals that they come across. It is easier for them to hunt weak animals than healthy ones. When you are at vulnerable points in your life, you will have a hard time escaping the predatory methods of a wolf.

Over and over I tell people who are divorcing, beware of getting involved in a relationship—you aren't in a healthy place. You are vulnerable of becoming the next prey of a self-absorbed Wolf. Often times my advice is ignored. I have even ignored my own advice, because I didn't understand my own vulnerability. After a major loss, your vulnerability is easy for a self-absorbed Wolf to not only spot but easily identify your emotional needs.

Soon after my divorce, I started "dating" a man off and on for three years. It wasn't until I got my head screwed on straight that I was able to see what was going on. I had exchanged one breed of Wolf for another. I delayed my healing process, consequently bringing more pain on myself. Throughout this time of my life, I am sure I neglected the needs of my daughter because I was so distracted. Likewise, I drove my friends crazy as I denied their cautionary advice. Amazingly God, in His mercy and truth of Romans 8:28, *"took all things and worked them together for good."* He refined my life. I learned that I had been seeking human relationships to meet something that only He could meet. When we look to other humans as our primary source of having needs met, we are setting ourselves up for disappointment. God never designed things for one person to meet all our needs. He designed things for Him to be the provider of our needs. We become self-absorbed in our pursuit to get our needs met, and in our weakness, we become prey to Wolves. I wouldn't understand the allure and trickery truths of Wolves if I hadn't been in their grips. God spared me and God can spare you!

In the animal kingdom, wolves come in different varieties. A brief search on the internet reveals two main types of wolves; red and grey. The red and grey wolves have many differences (size, food habitat), but they also have many common characteristics. This is also the case for self-absorbed Wolves. They come in three types; addicted, controlling, and narcissistic. All three types of self-absorbed wolves have things in common, but they display themselves differently and have different capacities for change. Only time, God, and wise counsel will help you understand what kind of Wolf is in your life and what their capacity for change really is.

Labeling someone a Wolf is a very serious thing and should not be done lightly. The reality is that only God knows a man's heart (1 Samuel 16:7). We live in an incredibly self-absorbed society, one groomed in "me first." The role models of today are making tons of money off of reality shows that glorify putting "me first." When working with cases that involve potential Wolves, there are several underlying questions that need to be considered. Is the person's Wolf behavior a learned behavior that they can unlearn? Was this person so deprived of their emotional needs as a child that they are stunted in their emotional development? Is this person just being incredibly self-absorbed due to wanting to do life their own way? Is this person a diagnosable Narcissist thereby having little hope for change? How capable of change is this person? How willing is this person to attempt to make change? If they don't change, one can't assume they are a Narcissist because maybe the person chose not to change. If they do change, one can't say for sure that they aren't a Narcissist because in the short-term, a Narcissist can put on a great act. In reality, only time reveals the truth. There are also valid psychological exams that determine a person's level of Narcissism, but good luck trying to get a Narcissist to take one.

For the sake of not seeing a Narcissistic Wolf in every corner, I am going to refer to a Narcissistic Wolf Continuum (see Figure 4). The continuum goes from left to right; selfless, self-absorbed seasons or developmental phases, self-absorbed problems, characteristics of Narcissism, and finally on the far right, Narcissistic Personality Disorder.

The Narcissistic Wolf Continuum

Selfless	Self-absorbed Seasons	Self-absorbed	Features	Narcissistic
	Seasons -	Addictions	Narcissism	Personality
	After Divorce	Controlling		Disorder
	Death of loved one			
	Development -			
	Two Year Olds			
	Teenagers			

Figure 4

Selfless Side of the Continuum

On the Narcissistic Wolf Continuum, selflessness is to the far left. The only person who ever walked on Earth and lived this side of the continuum was Jesus. The more we allow God to transform us into Christ's image, the closer we walk to this side of the continuum. Remember 1st Corinthians 13:4-7 illustrates love in its purest, most unconditional form. There is no thought of self in this kind of love, and it is only derived from a relationship with God. In Max Lucado's book, *A Love Worth Giving[9]*, he states, "A marriage-saving love is not within us. A friendship-preserving devotion cannot be found in our hearts. We need help from an outside source. A transfusion. Would we love as God loves? Then we start by receiving God's love".

During life we get only glimpses of this pure, unconditional love. In recent times, Mother Teresa was, in my opinion, the person who came closest to embodying unconditional, sacrificial love for the world to see. Another glimpse of love comes to us when we become parents. There are moments in parenting where you make sacrifices for your child that you wouldn't make for any other person. In fact, the national average in 2004 of raising a child to the age of 18 is as follows: if the families income was less than $41,700 annually the cost was $134,370, if the families income was between $41,700-$70,200 the cost was $184,320, and if the families income was over $70,200 the average cost of raising a child was $269,520[10]. Those numbers alone are telling of the sacrifices a parent makes in order to raise a child. Our children also have an amazing capacity to express love to us. How many times do they forgive our failings as a parent?

Other glimpses of love exist in many aspects of our lives. What about the glimpse of love we experience when we are fall in love? Do you remember all the sacrifices you made while you pursued love? Imagine the amount of money you spent on dates, clothing, and your cellular bill, not to mention the lack of sleep.

In these glimpses of love, what is missing is the purity of unconditional love. There are hidden motivations in each of these types of love. For the parent, there is an expectation of how their child should behave. For the lover, there is a hope of returned love. For the child, there is a deep need for acceptance and love from their parents. I remember when my daughter was a toddler, she would literally come up to me, and put her arms up, and say, "preciate Amanda," which was her way of saying that she needed me to take time to appreciate and spend time with her. She was learning to ask for what she needed. I can only hope each time she asked, I met her need.

Self-Absorbed Seasons/Development:

We all suffer from self-absorption at different times in our lives. In fact, during certain times of the developmental phases, self-absorption is normal. A two year old who says "mine," who wants what they want when they want it, and who throws temper tantrums when they don't is being normal! A teenager, who thinks of himself first, who believes the world revolves around him, who can suck you dry and then ask for more is being normal! These are typical developmental seasons of life. The process is teaching the individual how recognize their needs by making them overtly noticeable. Then hopefully with love and understanding, the parent guides the child in how to manage these needs and how to have them met in healthy ways. Sadly, when parents react to these normal developmental stages out of their own selfishness, children don't learn how to manage their own needs. When an adult says "mine," wants what she wants when she wants it, throws temper tantrums, thinks only of herself, and believes the world revolves around her, she is being self-absorbed!

When someone is newly divorced and still grieving their marriage, they have little to give. When someone is grieving the loss of a loved one, they have little to give. When someone is battling a chronic or terminal illness, they have little to give. During these seasons of life, a person will be more self-absorbed in their struggle to survive. Galatians 6:2 tells us that we are to carry our own loads, but that we are to carry each other's burdens.

These developmental phases and seasons of life will come and go. They will eventually resolve themselves and hopefully the end result is a person who is more giving as a result of having walked through them successfully.

The Self-Absorbed Wolf-side of the Continuum:

The self-absorbed side of the continuum is where you start seeing Wolf-like behavior. The measure for traversing from the left to the right side of the continuum is how frequently a person's self-absorbed behavior neglects and disregards another person's needs or well-being.

All Wolf types have controlling tendencies at their core, whether they are the addicted Wolf, the controlling Wolf, or the narcissistic Wolf. Wolves have an insatiable necessitation to meet their needs and to protect themselves, no matter the cost to others, including those they "love." If you have ever been in a relationship with a person who has self-absorbed tendencies, you will recognize your feelings in the following list:

George R. Bach and Ronald M. Deutsch, in their book, *Stop! You're Driving Me Crazy[11]* (1980, pps72 – 273)

1. Feeling temporarily thrown off balance and momentarily unable to right oneself.
2. Feeling lost, not knowing where to turn, searching aimlessly.
3. Being caught off guard.
4. Feeling disconnected, confused, disoriented.
5. Feeling off balance, as if the rug had been pulled from under one's feet.

6. Receiving double messages but somehow unable or fearful to ask for clarification.
7. Feeling generally "bugged" by the simple presence of a person
8. To discover the one was mistaken in one's evaluation of where one stood or what it was all about.
9. Feeling totally unprepared for a broken promise or unfulfilled expectation.
10. Experiencing the shattering of an important "dream."
11. Where one assumed goodwill, ill will seems to prevail.
12. One feels pushed around, not in control of one's own direction.
13. Unable to get off redundantly spinning circles of thoughts.
14. What seems clear becomes muddled.
15. An uneasy, weird feeling of emptiness.
16. A strong wish to get away, yet feeling unable to move, as if frozen.
17. One is befuddled, not able to attack the problem.
18. Feeling vaguely suspicious that something is wrong.
19. Feeling that one's subjective world has become chaotic. (272 & 272)

While the reactions of being with all three wolves may have similarities, there are many differences that are worth discussing.

The Addicted Wolf

The Addicted Wolf can be addicted to a wide variety of substances; food, alcohol, drugs, sex, work, love, and shopping. The addicted wolf starts off as the "fun guy." He is the life of the party! In the midst of all the fun, it is really easy not to notice the addictive patterns since he is a master of deflection. Oftentimes, as an addictive person is falling in love they may rely less on their substance of choice. This tendency has biological and psychological roots. During this time, the brain undergoes a chemical reaction that releases phenylethylamine, or PEA. PEA is an endogenous neuroamin, meaning it increases attention and activity in animals. Researchers have discovered through brain scans that when a person is experiencing romantic attraction, certain pockets of the brain are activated that have a high concentration of receptors for dopamine, the chemical messenger closely tied to states of euphoria, craving and addiction[12]. The Addicted Wolf's pursuit of love temporarily satisfies his cravings for alcohol or whatever other substance they are addicted to.

The science of addictions has its own continuum of whether someone is classified as a user, abuser, or addict. What is important to our discussion is the self-absorption of the behavior and the inability to self-reflect on how that behavior affects others.

For instance, someone who doesn't have any issues with food will eat on a regular basis, not spend a lot of time thinking about food, and have a nonchalant attitude toward food. This person has a lot of time to think about other things and give their attention to others. A person who is moving up on the continuum of food being an "issue," whether it is binge eating or self-deprivation, may spend more time thinking about food or trying not to think about food, craving food or ignoring their cravings, planning what they are going to eat or calculating how to reduce their calories. Food is always on their mind.

Regardless of their substance of choice, the Addicted Wolf's life is consumed by their addiction. Their lives revolve around that addiction, rather than being involved in and caring for the needs of those around them. They live in a land of never ending cycles. For a person suffering from bulimia, their cycle can be triggered by a negative event, and they will start planning their binge. Then they will eat with compulsive repetition to numb out their feelings, after which they will purge to get ride of all the bad food they ate. Next, they will feel consumed with guilt and shame, and the next binge may start just to expel the feelings of culpability from the first binge. Can you image how much time is taken up in the mind of an addict? I remember working with Mary who suffered from Bulimia. Mary described a binge where she set her four year old in front of the television with a video before she stated her binge. In Mary's mind, this was taking care of her child first. Mary then proceeded to binge on cereal. When her child asked for cereal, Mary redirected the child back to the video and continued her binge. When I asked Mary about the developmental process of a four year old wanting to be with mommy and have cereal like mommy, Mary was able to realize her self-absorption in the moment. Today Mary is living free from binges and purges. She is working towards incorporating healthy eating into her family's life. She makes sure she makes intentional efforts at paying attention to her children's emotional needs. There are still days her bulimic Wolf tries to draw her away from dealing with the realities of life, but she presses forward despite those urges.

Oftentimes addictions start during adolescence. Recall that the normal development of an adolescent is having ever-present needs. If a child is growing up in a home where the parents are self-absorbed and unavailable to meet their needs, an addiction becomes a convenient way to numb the real needs neglected by the parent. I heard a speaker say once that a teenager has one of two choices if his or her parents are neglecting their teen's emotional needs: an addiction or suicide. What a sad choice!

In Elan Golumb's book, *Trapped In the Mirror[13]*, she discusses the effects of growing up with a narcissistic parent and how an addiction becomes a means of coping with the emotional neglect. She says, *"Because addiction keeps us from dealing with our problems (while creating others), we need progressively more of the drug as unattended problems increase and pull us down. Rather than suffer, we increasingly turn to what makes us feel good and forget. We get further away from the knowledge of self that would set us free." (155).*

I remember working with Rebecca, who was recovering from alcoholism. She was telling me how even amidst her addiction she managed to still be a good mom. I looked at her in surprise and said "Really, you believe that?" I then went over an example she had given me in the past where her nine year old daughter would come home from school and find her passed out.

Marj: "So, remember the afternoons, where you were passed out at home and didn't go get your daughter"

Rebecaa: "Yeah, she knew if I wasn't at the school she was supposed to walk home."

Marj: "Did you always pick her up when you were sober?"

Rebecca: "Usually, unless I had a meeting"

Marj: "Did she know on those days that you had a meeting and would be late?"

Rebecca: "Yes"

Marj: "So, the only times you didn't pick her up, without her knowing ahead of time that you might be late because of a meeting is when you had been drinking and were passed out at home."

Rebecca: "I guess that would be right."

Marj: "So, what do you think your daughter was thinking about on her walk home."

Rebecca: "She was probably wondering whether I had been drinking or not."

Marj: "So, whose need do you think came first, your daughter's security need in having a ride home or your drinking?"

The reality of the self-absorption of Rebecca's addiction sank in. She was able to see that it would be impossible for her to identify certain needs in her child while she had been actively drinking. In Rebecca's recovery, she was able to see the importance of reinforcing security back into her child by picking her up from school everyday. Rebecca has been free from the alcoholic Wolf within her for three years. She is intentionally paying attention to her daughter's emotional needs. When her daughter's past insecurities haunt her, Rebecca nurtures her and takes care of her daughter's emotional needs.

The movie *Spanglish[14]* does an amazing job of showing how the addiction cycle affects the family. In the film, the grandmother is an active alcoholic living with her daughter's family. One morning the grandmother is in the kitchen telling stories of the grand old days holding a glass of alcohol. Her daughter walks in and says, "Mother, before noon?" As the grandmother gets ready to defend herself, the clock strikes noon, and she toasts her daughter instead.

Throughout the movie, we see the incredible self-absorption of the daughter, Debra. She neglects her husband, is consumed with "encouraging" her thirteen year old daughter to lose weight, and later has an affair. During the movie, the grandmother goes into recovery, and Debra continues to blame her mother for her personal issues and her feelings of neglect as a child. The grandmother acknowledges the neglect and the mistakes she has made. She then helps Debra understand that she is an adult who has the choice to either move past her mother's mistakes and grow up or continue to let the past ruin her life.

The irony through the whole movie is through another character, a single parent mother who makes sacrifice after sacrifice for what is in the best interest of her child. It is a stark comparison to the picture of an "ideal family" with all the hidden self-absorption. Self-absorption affected the whole family's functioning.

Addictions take time! All the time spent avoiding feelings and living in a never-ending cycle of the addiction, keeps the addict very busy. If you think about it, they really are too consumed and busy with their own stuff to think about how much time they have available to live out 1st Corinthians 13. It will and it does affect their relationship with others. Let's take a closer look at what the addicted Wolf is ignoring when it comes to the love of 1st Corinthians 13...

If *love never gives up*, how does an Addicted Wolf explain "numbing" him or herself from problems?

If *love cares more for others than for self,* how does the Addicted Wolf explain all the time and money spent on their addiction, rather than on others?

If *love doesn't want what it doesn't have*, how does the Addicted Wolf explain the insatiable cravings for his or her substance of choice?

If *love doesn't have a swelled head,* how does the Addicted Wolf explain all the times he or she has blamed others for his or her problems?

If *love doesn't force itself on others,* how does the Addicted Wolf explain his or her insistence on doing what he or she needs to do to have access to their addictive substance? Oftentimes, Addicted Wolves will use manipulation to get what they want.

If *love isn't always "me first,"* how does the Addicted Wolf explain the times he or she forgot to do something or was unavailable because of the addiction?

If *love doesn't fly off the handle,* how does the Addicted Wolf explain the angry rages, either when they were intoxicated or when they weren't able to drink like they wanted to?

If *loves doesn't keep score of the sins of others,* why doesn't the Addicted Wolf deal with the problems that are before them rather than using their addiction to numb the pain?

If *love doesn't revel when others grovel,* how can the Addicted Wolf be so sarcastic and insinuate that the other never does enough?

If *love takes pleasure in the flowering of truth,* why does the Addicted Wolf have such a hard time admitting he or she has a problem?

If *love puts up with anything,* how come the Addicted Wolf is always trying to escape in his or her addiction?

If *love trusts God always,* how come the Addicted Wolf turns to his or her addiction more than God?

If *love always looks for the best,* how come the Addicted Wolf can't look within themselves?

If *love never looks back,* how come the Addicted Wolf is so afraid to be sober?

If *love keeps going to the end,* how come the Addicted Wolf drinks? Binges/purges or starves? Looks at pornography? Works to the neglect of those closest to him or her?

My dear friend, there is NO DOUBT, the Addicted Wolf in your life is in a lot of pain, but they have to turn to God first before they can learn to love you like you deserve to be loved. There are core issues an Addicted Wolf must face and recovery is a slow, deliberate process. If you are in God's way, you need to move out of His way. Your involvement in trying to fix your spouse may in fact be its own addiction called codependency. Codependency is a compulsion to focus on other people's problems instead of your own. In an attempt to control the other person's addictive behaviors, like dumping out bottles of alcohol, you are covertly enabling their behavior. This only encourages the Wolf to go and purchase more alcohol. Instead, you should be focusing in on why you are trying to fix the other person. Codependent Wolves aren't loving unconditionally, they are loving conditionally with the hope of change. Oftentimes, in their attempt to fix their spouse's addiction, they are neglectful of the emotional needs of their children. It may be worth re-reading this section to reflect on your own behavior and how consumed you have been in regards to fixing your spouses problem.

The Controlling Wolf

The Controlling Wolf always starts off as a really "nice guy." Over time, the Controlling Wolf's nature reveals itself in the intimacy of a relationship. In *The Verbally Abusive Relationship[15]*, Patricia Evans describes why it is hard to recognize the verbal abuse of a controller. *"First, it is done mostly in secret, where only the partner of the verbal abuse hears it, or later understands its intent. Second, the verbal abuse become more intense over time and the partner becomes used to it and adapts to it. Third, the verbal abuse takes on many forms and disguises. And, finally, the controller is consistently discounting the partner's perception of reality."* (23)

The sad reality is that Controlling Wolves don't realize they are controlling. They perceive the world from only one perspective—theirs. Think of a person who sees the world through only black and white, as if no other colors exist. Can you image trying to explain to them what the color blue looks like? In the movie, *Pleasantville[16]*, a boy is transported into his favorite black and white television show where everyone does the same thing and nothing ever changes. Nobody thinks for themselves and everything appears perfect. Then his sister, who has a mind of her own, also ends up in Pleasantville and introduces a different perspective. Color literally starts to spread throughout their black and white world. People are terrified of the color they have never seen before. Color becomes bad.

Controlling Wolves don't grasp the concept of color or another person's perspective. Rather than questioning what they might be lacking, the Controlling Wolf will assume you are lacking! This means that trying to explain the other colors of the rainbow to the Wolf is futile. The Controlling Wolf is unable to grasp the concept. In fact, the Controlling Wolf sees another perspective as a threat to his or her existence.

Controlling Wolves roam the world assuming they have the "right" view and anyone who doesn't concur with their view is just a "stupid sheep." Controlling Wolves don't marry other Controlling Wolves; they marry naive sheep. They perceive the sheep as something they can mold and shape, something they can devour. A Wolf does not see a sheep as its equal!

Patricia Evans[17] refers to the controller as an abuser. *"The abuser knows no Personal Power, nor does he experience the security and self-acceptance of Personal Power. Consequently, he avoids his feelings of powerlessness by dominating and controlling his partner. The abuse is determined not to admit to his manipulation and control. If he did, he would come face to face with his own feelings. The abuser rejects his partner's warmth and openness, because these are the very qualities which he fears in himself...these qualities mean vulnerability, and...vulnerability is tantamount to death"* (39 & 40)

The book of Proverbs also has a lot to say about controlling wolves...*"If you reason with an arrogant cynic, you'll get slapped in the face; confront bad behavior and get a kick in the shin. So don't waste your time on a scoffer; all you'll get for your pains is abuse."* Proverbs 9:7 & 8

"Don't accept a meal from a tightwad; don't expect anything special. He'll be as stingy with you as he is with himself; he'll say, "Eat! Drink!" but won't mean a word of it. His miserly serving will turn your stomach when you realize the meal's a sham." Proverbs 23:8

Controlling Wolves oftentimes have huge money issues! Jenny described how her husband gave her a 600 dollar monthly budget for food, household cleaning supplies, and personal hygiene products for a family of five, while he earned more than $100,000 a year. Can you imagine? Maybe in the 1980's this would have worked but certainly this budget is now unrealistic and obsolete. She had to put everything on a credit card (that gained points) and where every penny would be accounted for. She was given $65.00 for her own spending money per month. Furthermore, a Controlling Wolf doesn't follow his or her own rules. Jenny's husband spent $100,000 on the landscaping, while she juggled a monthly household budget of $600.

In Luke, Jesus has a lot to say about the controlling wolves of the time: the Pharisees. *"What can I say about such men?" Jesus asked. "With what shall I compare them? They are like a group of children who complain to their friends, 'You don't like it if we play "wedding" and you don't like it if we play "funeral" ' For John the Baptist used to go without food and never took a drop of liquor all his life and you said, 'He must be crazy' But I eat my food and drink my wine, and you say, 'What a glutton Jesus is? And he drinks! And has the lowest sort of friends! But I am sure you can always justify your inconsistencies."* Luke 7:31-35

Another client, April, described how when she and her future husband, Bryan, were dating in college, he would call and ask her if she wanted to go to a movie or dinner? The woman perceived this as a choice, not as a red flag. April rationalized and defended Bryan's behavior, saying he was on a limited budget. I asked April the following questions to help her understand Bryan's controlling tendencies.

Marj: "Let's say that you are the parent of a two year old and you want the child to drink milk so they get their recommended allowance of calcium. Do you, as a parent, know what is in the best interest of a two year old?"

April: "Of course, I am the parent, and they are the child."

Marj: "Now if you ask a toddler to drink his/her milk, what would the response be of a typical two year old?"

April: "Probably, NO, because two years—old like that word."

Marj: "What if you asked your toddler if they wanted their milk in a Barney cup or a Spongebob cup?"

April: "They would pick one of the cups."

Marj: "So the issue wouldn't be about milk. You would have been controlling their need for milk, but still letting them have a choice in the cup."

April: "Right, so maybe Bryan was just looking out for my best interest."

Marj: "It is one thing for a parent to developmentally know what is in their child's best interest. It is entirely another thing for an adult to presume to know what is in the best interest. Bryan only gave you a choice of movie or dinner, he didn't give you any other options or ask if you had other preferences."

April: "Okay, so what would an equal relationship look like in that situation. What should I be looking for?"

Marj: "He probably would have said something like, 'Hey I have $25.00 a week to do fun stuff. Tell me what kind of stuff you like to do? I want to be able to figure out how to make those things happen.' You would also then want to find out what he likes to do and also make sure his preferences are also considered."

Controlling Wolves aren't thinking about what is best for everybody! They are thinking about themselves! I love Charles Swindoll's depiction of Abigail in 1 Samuel 25 from his book *Fascinating Stories of Forgotten Lives[18]*. She was married to a man named Nabal, which is the Hebrew word for "fools" It is also the word used for churlish, rude, ignorant, dishonest, belligerent, obstinate, and stupid.

A summary of the story reveals that Nabal was a wealthy land owner. David, the future king of Israel, provided security from thieves and wild animals to the land owners. Nabal refused to acknowledge David's services or to pay for them. David's response to this unpaid debt was going to be heavy handed. One of Nabal's servants overheard, and rather than confronting the "fool," he went to Nabal's wife, Abigail, and told her what happened. The servant describes the dilemma to Abigail and then said, ..."*Now therefore, know and consider what you should do, for evil is plotted against our master and against all his household; and he is such a worthless man that no one can speak to him.*" 1 Samuel 25:17

Swindoll, then summarizes with this thought;

"How tragic it is to live under the authority of a person who won't listen and doesn't even have his servants' respect. Do you live with someone like that? Were you reared by a mother or father who simply could not be wrong? Do you have a grown child, now an adult, who will not listen? Do you have a spouse who is completely out of touch with how he or she affects others? If so, then you understand why that is one of the most difficult situations in life to endure. You can't get through to them. You know before you begin to communicate that they're going to shut out your words. And they have a dozen reasons why what you say is wrong. Nabals exist today." (140 & 141)

If you are married to a Controlling Wolf, you know the dilemma that Abigail and the servant faced. Nabal cared more about not spending money on security and went so far as to deny the existence of the service, and in doing so put his family and servants at risk.

Controlling Wolves will put your life at risk! They are fools, not known for respecting wisdom, as it is often different than their desire. Let's look at the wisdom of 1Cornthians 13.

If *love never gives up*, how does a Controlling Wolf refuse to negotiate or consider another's need or perspective?

If *love cares more for others than for self*, how does a Controlling Wolf insist on his/her way or the highway?

If *love doesn't want what it doesn't have*, how does a Controlling Wolf demand his/her way?

If *love doesn't have a swelled head*, how does a Controlling Wolf believe that he/she has the truth or the "right" way of thinking?

If *love doesn't force itself on others*, how does the Controlling Wolf continually demand his/her own way?

If *love isn't always "me first"*, how does the Controlling Wolf look to his needs and neglect the needs of others?

If *love doesn't fly off the handle*, how does a Controlling Wolf explain his/her anger outbursts as a means of getting what they want?

If *loves doesn't keep score of the sins of others*, how come the Controlling Wolf is pointing out the faults of others?

If *love doesn't revel when others grovel*, how come a Controlling Wolf tells you "I told you so"?

If *love takes pleasure in the flowering of truth*, how come a Controlling Wolf can't see another person's perspective?

If *love puts up with anything*, how is it that the Controlling Wolf spends so much time criticizing the way their spouse does things wrong?

If *love trusts God always*, how come a Controlling Wolf won't surrender control to God?

If *love always looks for the best*, how come a Controlling Wolf can see the faults of other's so easily and quickly point them out?

If *love never looks back*, how come the Controlling Wolf is consumed by fear?

If *love keeps going to the end*, why does a Controlling Wolf will go to their end rather another's or God's?

I want you to grasp the intensity of change that will be needed for a Controlling Wolf to change. First, the Controlling Wolf has to be willing to become a sheep! Can you imagine how fearful this would be? The Controlling Wolf not only has to surrender to God's control, but he or she surrenders to being a sheep, and this is less than a Wolf in a Wolf's perspective. The Controlling Wolf will know there are other Controlling Wolves out their and he/she is choosing to be a sheep. Do you remember in John 3, the Pharisee named Nicodemus who came to visit Jesus in the dark of the night. He was beginning to understand that Jesus was the son of God. But, he had to surrender his safe world of being a Pharisee. Jesus was telling him he had to be born again. There is a huge amount of vulnerability that takes place as a Controlling Wolf understands his own nature and realizes that he must be born again. God's grace is always sufficient, but a controlling Wolf has to step into complete and total surrender and let God do the transformation!

The Narcissistic Wolf

The Narcissistic Wolf is the most dangerous of all on the self-absorption continuum. There are very subtle differences in the Narcissistic Wolf as compared to the Controlling Wolf or the Addicted Wolf. Only time reveals the true nature of a Narcissistic Wolf. And by time, I mean years. In *Bold Love[19]*, Allendar & Longman describes the difference between a fool and an evil person, "*In many respects, an evil person is simple a more severe fool who has progressed to a level of foolishness that is deeply severed from human emotion (empathy and shame) and human involvement (devouring destruction). An evil person is more crafty and deceitful fool who is more artful at escaping exposure. Further, an evil person delights in the destructive thrill of controlling and then consuming his victim.*" (257)

Narcissistic Wolves are masters at creating perceptions of reality. They are able to morph quite easily into whatever they want. They are constantly reinventing themselves with each new experience. If they are getting too close to being exposed, they have a wide variety of tactics available to them. As a Christian, one has to always believe in miracles or the possibility of change, but change for a full-blown narcissistic Wolf would indeed be nothing short of a miracle. To this day, science still inconclusively debates on the curability of Narcissistic Personality Disorder.

The best place to start in understanding the Narcissistic Wolf is to look at the criteria that define Narcissistic Personality Disorder (NPD) in the DSM IV TR[20], a reference book which defines mental health diagnosis. First, there is a broad category that explains NPD as a pervasive pattern of grandiosity, (in fantasy or behavior), a need for admiration, and a lack of empathy, beginning by early adulthood and present in a variety of contexts, as indicated by five or more of the following:

1.**has a grandiose sense of self-importance (exaggerates achievements and talents, expects to be recognized as superior without commensurate achievements)**

A Narcissistic Wolf is almost always in some sort of limelight. They are the "it" person! Everyone loves them, but no one is really close to them. People want to be close to them, but the grandiose sense of self keeps a very restricted view of who they can associate with. I am not saying that everyone in the limelight is a Narcissistic Wolf, but one does need to be more on guard in this arena.

2.**is preoccupied with fantasies of unlimited success, power, brilliance, beauty, or ideal love**

A Narcissistic Wolf is always on the search for the next BIG thing. It could be the next big deal. It could be the next big relationship. It could be the next big whatever. Again, not all people who have reached success, power, brilliance, beauty, or ideal love are Narcissistic Wolves. Remember it is the exaggeration of the achievements or talent. One Narcissistic Wolf I know bought a doctorate degree on line, and then proceeded to represent himself as a clinical psychologist and even wore a lab coat with a stethoscope when working with his patients. When he got caught, he said he thought his experience afforded him the title of Doctor. In a blog comment on the article that exposed him, someone with personal details of the "doctors' life was quoted as saying "On to bigger and better things."

If you have become a number one selling artist you are not exaggerating your talent. However, living in an environment where everyone wants to know you, everyone wants to associate with you, and everyone jumps when you snap your fingers, gives you a lot of power, and one can easily begin to believe all the hoopla.

3.**believes that he or she is "special" and unique and can only be understood by, or should associate with, other special or high-status people (or institutions)**

A Narcissistic Wolf is very selective about who they hang out with! They believe they are better than others. Some Narcissistic Wolves are very arrogant and easy to spot. The wiser Narcissistic Wolves give the appearance of humility and are much more cunning. They may at times hang out with people "lower" than them, but it is about making themselves look good in some way, not about valuing the person for who they are.

4.**requires excessive admiration**

Narcissistic Wolves feed off the admiration of others. It is a lifeline for them. People with Narcissistic Personality Disorder have been referred to as werewolf—they require the "blood" of others to survive. Admiration is essential for them. Maybe that is why Saul's jealousy of the attention David was receiving led him to wanting David dead. Maybe that is why King Herod couldn't allow another person to be a king, so he had every Jewish boy under the age of two murdered.

5.**has a sense of entitlement (unreasonable expectations of especially favorable treatment or automatic compliance with has or her expectations)**

Narcissistic Wolves live by "my way or the highway" and "I want what I want when I want it". They may have this attitude overtly like a general in the military, where compliance is expected and no questions are to be asked. Or, they may covertly manipulate situations to go their way. Oftentimes, it is this sense of entitlement can bring on a narcissistic rage. Do you recall King Saul's relentless pursuit of David? Do you recall King Herod's relentless pursuit of the new king who had been born to the Jews? Do you recall Queen Jezebel's relentless pursuit of Elijah? ALL of these describe a narcissistic rage. Narcissists are inexorable in their pursuit of anyone who threatens their finely tuned perspective.

6.**is interpersonally exploitive (takes advantage of others to achieve his or her own ends)**

Narcissistic Wolves are always about what is in it for me. There is no end to the amount of strategizing they do to achieve their desires. They are master chess players, calculating every move in a relationship, strategically weighing the costs and benefits. The concept of self-sacrifice is foreign to them. The concept of other's sacrifice for them is expected, yet unappreciated.

7.**lacks empathy: is unwilling to recognize or identify with the feelings and needs of others**

Narcissistic Wolves lack empathy. Caution: some Narcissistic Wolves are able to give the appearance of empathy when it makes them look good or feel good. The true test is: when they are in a mutually dependent relationship, are they able to show empathy for the other person's perspective? Even when it conflicts with their own needs being met? If your spouse lacks empathy, but doesn't meet the criteria for a Narcissist, it may be wise to consider other mental health issues, such as Asperger's Syndrome.

8.**is often envious of others or believes that others are envious of the**

Think of a pair of two year olds playing together. Which toy do they want to play with? The toy the other two year old has. Narcissistic Wolves want what the other person has. They are not satisfied with what they have. They always want more! If they happen to be the person who has the most, then they assume others want to be like them.

9.**shows arrogant haughty behaviors or attitudes**

We all can easily pick out a person who is haughty and proud; however, not all arrogant people are narcissists. Arrogance is definitely a caution sign to pay attention to. An arrogant or prideful heart is a heart that isn't fully surrendered to God. This a visible sign, which is why Narcissistic Wolves who give the appearance of humility are harder to identify.

Remember, to be diagnosed with a Narcissistic Personality Disorder, at least *five* of the above categories must consistently describe the person's interactions. There are a variety of scientific testing models for determining if someone has NPD and to what degree they have it. However, it is rare that a narcissist will be willing to take a personality test. I truly believe the words of 1 Samuel 16:7, “only God knows the heart of a man.” Only God knows the capacity of a person’s willingness or capacity to change. A person’s actions may be narcissistic, but judgment should be reserved for God. You shouldn’t jump to the conclusion that your spouse has NPD; however, the further someone’s behavior is on the self-absorbed continuum, the more they act like a Narcissist. Once again, let’s look at the wisdom of 1 Corinthians 13 to define what selfless love looks like as opposed to self-absorbed Wolf.

If *love cares more for others than for self,* how does a Narcissistic Wolf explain his or her lack of empathy for those closest to him or her?

If *love doesn’t want what it doesn’t have*, how does the Narcissistic Wolf explain its insatiable appetite for more?

If *love doesn’t have a swelled head*, how does the Narcissistic Wolf explain his or her arrogance?

If *love doesn’t force itself on others*, how does the Narcissistic Wolf explain his or her manipulation?

If *love isn’t always “me first”*, how does the Narcissistic Wolf explain the unmet needs around him or her?

If *love doesn’t fly off the handle*, how does the Narcissistic Wolf explain his or her rage?

If *loves doesn't keep score of the sins of others*, how does the Narcissistic Wolf explain his or her list of wrongs that he or she keeps about those closest to them?

If *love doesn't revel when others grovel*, how is it that a Narcissistic Wolf craves the experience of being right?

If *love takes pleasure in the flowering of truth*, how is it that a Narcissistic Wolf attacks with such a vengeance when truth is exposed?

If *love puts up with anything*, how can the Narcissistic Wolf be so demanding of getting his or her way in his or her time?

If *love trusts God always*, how does the Narcissistic Wolf explain his or her lack of a heart surrendered to God?

If *love always looks for the best*, how can the Narcissistic Wolf explain his or her tendency to blame others?

If *love never looks back*, how does the Narcissistic Wolf keep track of the sins of others against him or her?

If *love keeps going to the end*, how does the Narcissistic Wolf explain the trail of destroyed lives behind him or her?

If *love never gives up*, how does a Narcissistic Wolf so easily transfer from one relationship to the next?

Whether you are dealing with an Addicted Wolf, a Controlling Wolf, or a Narcissistic Wolf, there are several key factors I have found to identify self-absorbed Wolves of any kind. They are most exposed in the context of their intimate relationships. They are unable to hold up their performance at home. Many things happen within the families of Wolves that are unseen by friends, neighbors, work, church, or the communities they live in. Oftentimes, if family members dare share with someone, that person often believes they are over reacting or over dramatizing. My own understanding of this problem began when I read Patricia Evan's primary consequences of verbal abuse in her book. *The Verbally Abusive Relationship[21].* I remember sitting at home after an encounter with my husband. I remember talking to my brother on the phone, and he asked me what was wrong. He told me that I was acting like I had just been hit. In that moment, I realized that I had just been verbally beaten up, and it was with those words that I headed to the bookstore and discovered her book. It was the first book I ever read that made a difference, and as I read through her symptom list, I suffered from almost every single one of the consequences of verbal abuse. I have since adapted her list to be utilized in marriages that have a self-absorbed Wolf lurking.

Incongruity in public verses home

The biggest evidence of incongruence is the presentation of the self-absorbed Wolf to the public verses how they behave at home. They have a well crafted disguise for public. In the church, Wolves have mastered what it looks like to be "righteous." They can quote Scripture. They can tell you wonderful stories. They can show up for ministry (remember they are benefiting from it...admiration, image management, snaring their prey). The truth is at home! What is their relationship like with their spouse? What is their relationship like with their children? Oftentimes if there is trouble at home, the self-absorbed Wolf has figured out how to make him or herself look like the good one.

It is typical for the spouse of a self-absorbed Wolf to suffer from anger issues and not understand why. There are so many unmet needs in the home of a Wolf that the family is looking for scraps wherever they can find them. These scraps show up in dysfunctional behaviors on the family's part such as behavioral problems in the children, like drugs or eating disorders. Spouses of Wolves can suffer from anxiety or depression and other health issues. Meanwhile the self-absorbed Wolf reinvents the picture to make himself or herself look like the victim and the one trying to fix everything. I have learned to proceed with great caution when I see a couple where one spouse is consumed with anger while the other spouse appears to be healthy.

Confusion

There are several things that contribute to the confusion in a relationship with a self-absorbed Wolf. The constant reinventing of the self creates a lot of confusion for those close to the Wolf. The Wolf is always shifting. Just when those close to the Wolf think they have it figured out, the wolf morphs into something else.

My client Rhonda told me a story about a Thanksgiving dinner with her new sister-in-law, Sylvia, who was a vegetarian and a dedicated animal lover. Sylvia's husband Bob, however, was an avid carnivore, so she decided to cook a real turkey, along with her tofu dish. At first glance, this appeared to be an act of respecting another's views on meat and accommodating them. During the prayer for dinner, Sylvia asked God to bless the animals that had sacrificed their lives for the dinner. There was more confusion when a second turkey's life was sacrificed as a center piece for the festive table. It was apparent to Rhonda that perception was more important to Sylvia than her value's system to the animal and every avid carnivore in the room was reminded of the sacrifice that had been made.

What you thought was true, isn't.

Because the self-absorbed Wolf is constantly reinventing himself or herself, there is a lot of lying. I have come to the conclusion that certainly some of the lying is intentional due to the self-absorbed Wolf's manipulation, but I also believe that the self-absorbed Wolf believes some of his or her lies in the process reinventing the truth. The spouse of a self-absorbed Wolf will oftentimes start feeling like they should get things in writing or that they should have a video camera. The constant switching of reality creates huge doubts in the perception of the spouse who is married to a self-absorbed Wolf. They have a hard time sorting through the web of deception that is constantly being woven.

Karen told me how a man she was dating was supposed to show up for her birthday party. Through out the evening of her party he kept calling with one excuse after another of why he was running late. First he had gotten off work late, then he had laid down for a nap, then he had to get his kids, then he encountered an accident and got delayed at the freeway. Finally at 10:30 p.m., he realized he wouldn't be able to get to her party. Ironically, the next day, Karen ran into the man's daughter. The daughter made some comment about her dad being late to get her because he had been at Karen's birthday party. Karen was in complete shock, and when she confronted the man about it, he shrugged it off and pretended that his daughter must have been confused.

Another client, Tiffany, told me of a difficult meeting she had with her divorced parents. The year prior, her father had committed to flying with her to college to register for her freshman classes, and then at the last minute, he cancelled due to a previous canoeing trip he had planned. Her mother made arrangements to take her there instead. This year as they were determining how to divide expenses for her second year of college, the previous registration trip came up. The father denied ever canceling and said he would never abandon his daughter like that. Tiffany was in shock. He asked Tiffany if she believed that this had happened. He asked his ex-wife if she really believed that doing something like that reflected his character. It didn't matter that there was evidence to the contrary. Sadly, I explained to Tiffany that it was highly probably her father believed he was telling the truth rather than lying. Self-absorbed Wolves twist the truth to live with themselves and they come to believe their twisting.

I can't quite put my finger on it!

When living with a Wolf, the other person is always looking for the answer to fix the problem that they can't quite figure out. You may have read countless self-help books, trying to figure out the situation, only to feel frustrated and more desperate. You may spend hours obsessing over what went wrong, what is wrong, what you can do differently and still not figure it out. And you truly believe that once you figure it out, it will be better. It is this unsolved puzzle that keeps you roped in. You feel like if you solve the puzzle, everything will finally fall into place. The problem is that your puzzle has a missing a piece! You just haven't figured that out yet.

Getting caught off guard

With all the inconsistency, manipulation, and deception, being caught off guard is a constant state. Just when you think you have seen it all, the self-absorbed wolf will surprise you with a new tactic. The words of a self-absorbed wolf in private can be brutal. The words of a self-absorbed Wolf in public are subtle (only you and the Wolf know the meaning behind what is said).

There will be incidents where you anticipate and prepare yourself for a bad reaction, only to get a positive response. There will be other incidents where you think you have done the right thing, and you will get a negative reaction. Anticipating a self-absorbed Wolf's next move is like playing chess. You must never forget that your opponent is a master in the game. Being wise in your countermoves is critical! In John Orberg's book, *At the End of the Game All the Pieces Go Back in the Box[22]*, tells a story of a painting called *Checkmate.* One day a master chess player was at the gallery where the painting was on display and stopped to look at it. After studying the chessboard on the painting he told his companion that the painting was incorrectly named as the person in checkmate still had one more move against his opponent. GOD always has one more move! Proverbs 23:6-8, warns us about becoming pawns of wolves; *"Don't associate with evil men; don't long for their favors and gifts. Their kindness is a trick; they want to use you as their pawn. The delicious food they serve will turn sour in your stomach and you will vomit it, and have to take back your words of appreciation for their 'kindness'."* (LB) Be aware, be on guard, and be wise!

Walking on egg shells

Anger is always just around the corner with a self-absorbed Wolf, and when it hits, it is like a tsunami. Anything that comes across its path will fall prey to its waves of rage! The amazing thing to me is that I have come to the conclusion that self-absorbed Wolves don't always remember their rage. Because of their constant shifting of the truth, they shift the rage out of the truth. If they do remember their rage, they blame it on whoever it was directed towards.

You can try all you want to have the house clean, the kids quiet, answer all his/her calls, and they may still come home and rage! The self-absorbed Wolf has a huge hole in their emotional needs bank that can never be filled by any human soul. And, the human soul who is trying to fill the emotional needs bank will be left with the feeling that no matter what they do it is never enough.

Vengeance is mine!

I have found that a key definer of the Narcissistic Wolf compared to the other types of Wolves is vengeance. I can't caution you enough about the reality of a Narcissistic Wolf's vengeance. When a Narcissistic Wolf feels like his "carefully tailored perception" is being attacked, he will relentlessly protect his image, even if it means destroying you in the process.

I remember Gail who worked in a church as a pastoral counselor. Soon after her divorce, she started dating a man (not a wise thing to do). After the end of their relationship, he started dating another woman who was in the process of a divorce. One day, when Gail was meeting with one of her lay leaders, she heard a story about this man dating one on the lay leader's friends who had been going through a divorce at the time. Gail became concerned as it appeared like he had a track record of dating women who were going through a divorce. Not realizing that she was dealing with a Narcissistic Wolf, she went to the man and confronted him. She still believed that if he realized his pattern, especially since he was now dating a woman who was not even divorced that he would stop. Little did Gail realize that she was exposing a self-absorbed Wolf. His attack became vicious. He rallied a group of supporters and went after her. He had people go to her boss and claim that she was "stirring up trouble." He had people go to the elders of the church and claim she was "crazy" and tried to get her fired. God protected her!

Sadly, I have had clients come into my office after nasty divorces where they have literally lost everything: their jobs, their finances, and the custody of their children, all because they didn't understand they had been up against a vengeful, Narcissistic Wolf.

Oftentimes, unsuspecting spouses or friends of Narcissistic Wolves will try to speak truth into the Wolf's life. Wolves don't like truth since it cracks their carefully constructed facade. If someone exposes too much of the Wolf's real self, the Wolf will attack that person with a vengeance. Telling a Narcissistic Wolf that he or she is a Narcissist is like telling Hugh Hefner that his multiple sex partners have been a wrong choice in his life.

Predictably, Unpredictable.

The reality is that self-absorbed Wolves have a chameleon nature to them. So, the "truth" as they see it or experience it is constantly shifting. In *The Verbally Abusive Relationship[23]*, one of the verbally abusive tactics of countering is discussed. Patricia Evans tells a story of a woman's interaction with her Controlling Wolf husband. Here the spouse has decided to just agree with the wolf no matter what he says.

"Ned: The lampshade doesn't go with the lamp.

Nan: Oh, yeah, the lampshade doesn't go with the lamp.

Ned: It does too go with the lamp.

Nan: Oh, the shade goes with the lamp.

Ned: You can't say it goes with it when the color's off.

Nan: Oh. I see, the color is off.

Ned: That's not what's wrong with it.

Nan: I'm trying to find out what you mean.

Ned: No, you're not. You're twisting my words around!" (91)

Can you see why figuring out where to put your finger would be impossible if the "truth" is constantly shifting. For those skeptics out there who think she should have called him on the carpet for his shifting perspective and claimed he just altered his opinion, there is always a price to pay with a Wolf regardless of how you react. Wolves only become predictable when you realize they are unpredictable, which means you can predict their unpredictability.

A growing sense that something is wrong with you

In your search to figure out what is wrong, you have come across many ideas that you have tried to implement. As I said before, these attempts have probably failed. The problem, however, isn't with your efforts; it is with your focus. You are trying to fix the wrong thing!

My dear reader, there is something wrong, but it's not what you think. You are trying to solve your problem with your spouse. You need to be solving your heart problem with God! In your attempts to figure out what is wrong, you have taken your focus off God and put your focus on fixing the problem.

This is where a professional counselor can help you. They will be able to look at your situation objectively and help you sort through the chaos. Not all professional counselors understand the effects a self-absorbed Wolf has on a relationship, so be wise in choosing a referral that will understand what is going on. I think it is also important to point out that not all pastors understand the nature of a self-absorbed Wolf. They may see the Wolf you are married to as a fine, upstanding Christian in the congregation, so be careful!

Desire to escape, run away, get away

Given the emotionally charged state of your marriage, it is no wonder you are exhausted and want to escape. I have heard many clients tell me that the easiest answer to their problem at home would be if their spouse died. Can you imagine how desperate someone would be to feel that way? Maybe you do.

The spouse of a self-absorbed Wolf often finds mini-escapes. For example, escape can be found in reading novels, shopping, eating, or even substance use. Unfortunately, none of these mini-escapes will help solve the problem! They instead increase the problem because the Wolf now has a new complaint and reason to point the finger at you! When you learn to escape by surrendering control to God, plan to be blamed for being too religious!

Questioning your own perception of reality. Only one truth exists—theirs.

It is a fact of nature that in many situations there are multiple truths; however, in a relationship with a self-absorbed Wolf, there is only one truth—theirs! Depending on how overtly or covertly controlling the self-absorbed Wolf is will affect your perception of reality.

Perceptions are just perceptions! In any situation, there are multiple experiences of what has unfolded. None of us are sovereign. None of us are able to see the whole picture, which is made up of many parts! In the self-absorbed Wolf's world, there is only one experience that is valid—theirs!

You can talk until you are blue in the face to try and have a self-absorbed Wolf see your perception, but you are wasting your breath! Proverbs 23:9 says, *"Don't waste your breath on a rebel. He will despise the wisest advice."* (LB)

Toward the end of my marriage, I started understanding that there was only one accurate perspective in my marriage according to my husband. I knew I needed to stop trying to explain, defend, and rationalize my perspective. We had a Pontiac Grand Am (which had a lot of emotional history and arguments from day one) that I believed needed to be sold. My husband, however, did not. Finally, we agreed to advertise it in the newspaper in order to sell it. One night while we were out we had a call on our answering machine with an offer. The next morning I asked my husband what he wanted to do about selling the car, he responded back by asking me what I wanted to do. In the past, I would have taken that as a legitimate question and given my perspective, I knew better. So, I said, "Do you want to know what I think or do you want me to just agree with what you think?" He actually admitted to wanting me to agree with his way of not selling the car. So instead of reacting with anger, instead of trying to convince him of why we should sell the car, I said that I didn't agree with his opinion and then took a leap of faith.

Remember the verse on submission? I said okay, we won't sell it and lifted the Grand Am's future up to God. For two years, I had the car, and it remained with me through the divorce settlement. I was so overwhelmed with life and readjusting to all the changes that the divorce had brought into my life that the Grand Am sat in my parking lot unused. I should have known that God had a purpose for my car, and this became clear when my brother, a single-parent college student, experienced the frustration of his car breaking down. I was able to give him the car, and realize that God had used my ex-husband's Wolf behavior of stubbornness for a greater good. I also learned that in submitting, I am submitting to God's greater good even if I couldn't see it. If I had insisted on my way, I would have missed out on a great learning experience of who God is and how He provides!

Your perception isn't wrong! It is only a perception. Your spouse's perception isn't wrong, it is only a perception. If your spouse is a self-absorbed Wolf though, they will only be able to tolerate one perception. Despite their inability to acknowledge more than one way, God is still sovereign! He is in control! He has a purpose! He will make a way! In His own time!

A double standard. Rules for you, different rules for your spouse.

There are two sets of standards in a home where there is a self-absorbed Wolf. Remember this standard will be constantly shifting. There is one standard that is set for other members in the family. Then there is the standard that is set for the self-absorbed Wolf. It is okay for the self-absorbed Wolf to be grumpy, moody, or angry; however, this behavior is not acceptable for anyone else in the family. It is okay for the self-absorbed Wolf to spend money on what he/she deems important and necessary. It is not okay for anyone else in the family to spend money in the ways they see fit.

In talking about Wolves, I fear that you will take your focus off what God needs to do in your life and focus on how horrible your self-absorbed Wolf treats you. Your transformation in this process is vital! In *Fascinating Stories of*

Forgotten Lives[24] by Chuck Swindoll, four plot lines of people's lives are described that provide wisdom in revealing a person's true heart. First, there are lives reflected by a racecar on a speedway. These are people who live life in the fast lane and occasionally stop at the pit to get fuel. At this quick pace, they accomplish very little and have minimal impact. When the race of life is over, they have an empty gas tank. Second, there are lives reflected by a meteor. These are people who rise to fame, and flash through the sky, and soon after, crash and burn. Third, there are the lives reflected by deep, quiet rivers. These are the people who are "consistent, giving, supportive, quietly powerful, and profoundly mysterious" (107 and 108). They are quiet and rarely make headlines, but they make a lasting impact on the world. Finally, there are the lives reflected by a roofline. "God has gifted this person with multiple talents, superior intellect, striking good looks, inner confidence, and every advantage for success." These people rise in leadership, but life eventually becomes unglued and their lives become characterized by "rebellion, scandal, disappointment, embarrassment, and complete failure."(108)

Which plot line do you want your life to parallel? I know I want my life to be a deep, quiet river that is formed by God. I want to rest in him regardless of the weather that sweeps across the banks of my life. When my life has floods from rapid rainfalls or melting snow, I want to rest in His provision and care.

Chapter IV
Beware of the Wolf Named King Herod

There are only two states of being: submission to God and goodness or the refusal to submit to anything beyond one's own will—which refusal automatically enslaves one to the forces of evil,
M. Scott Peck

Now that we have our eyes on Him, we can go back to understanding the nature of a self-absorbed Wolf. Matthew 2 reveals the nature of a very powerful Wolf who thought He could outwit a new King. *After Jesus was born in Bethlehem village, Judah territory – this was during Herod's kingship – a band of scholars arrived in Jerusalem from the East. They asked around, "Where can we find and pay homage to the newborn King of the Jews? We observed a star in the eastern sky that signaled his birth. We're on pilgrimage to worship him." (Matthew 2: 1&2 MSG).*

When word of their inquiry got to Herod, he was terrified - and not Herod alone, but most of Jerusalem as well. Herod lost no time. He gathered all the high priests and religious scholars in the city together and asked, "Where is the Messiah supposed to be born?" (Matthew 2:3&4 MSG)

*Herod then arranged a **secret meeting** with the scholars from the East. **Pretending to be as devout as they were**, he got them to tell him exactly when the birth-announcement star appeared. Then he told them the prophecy about Bethlehem, and said, "Go find this child. Leave no stone unturned. As soon as you find him, send word and **I'll join you at once in your worship**.?" (Matthew 2:7&8 MSG)*

King Herod moments are the ones that really catch you off guard. Don't ever minimize the amount of strategy, deception, and revenge a Wolf will employ in order to protect his or her perceived self-image. If the Wolf feels they are being attacked or threatened in any way, they will attack with vengeance. When Herod realized there was a new King on the horizon who would potentially become more popular and powerful than he was, he relentlessly pursued him. To eliminate this threat, King Herod attempted to find and destroy Jesus. When that didn't work, he had every baby under the age of two murdered, included his own son[25].

Remember who protected Jesus and his parents from King Herod's vengeance? GOD DID! King Herod had instructed the Three Wise Men to inform him of Jesus' location; however, God warned them not to report back to the king. Prior to King Herod's decree for young boys to be killed, God directed Joseph, in a dream, to flee Egypt. With their steps directed by God, Mary and Joseph left quietly and quickly in the middle of the night. They didn't confront the King; they didn't try to manage on their own! Rather, they rested in God's direction, care, and protection.

I have seen countless lives destroyed by modern day King Herods. Either the person didn't realize they were dealing with a Wolf in sheep's clothing, or they tried to battle the Wolf without waiting on God's direction. When you realize you are dealing with a potential Wolf, BEWARE. Remember Jesus understood that people would play by different rules than His. He also realized that these people would be present in the church. Matthew 10:16 MSG directs each of the disciples to be ***"Be as gentle as a dove and as cunning as a snake…when amidst wolves"***

Strategy 1 - PRAY.

Ask God for His wisdom. Ask God for His strength in your weakness. Ask God for His direction. Ask for His protection.

Strategy 2 – MEMORIZE SCIPTURES.

You are in a battle, and the Wolf isn't your only enemy. Your own negative thoughts can be your worst enemy. The Wolf has told you repeatedly who you should be and how you fail to measure up. You may have started to believe some of the things your Wolf has been telling you. The best line of defense is God's truth! When you are attacked with any thoughts or words by another that are negative, vengeful, or selfish, having scriptures memorized is the best way to counter the attack. Use this four step process to deal with the Wolf thoughts...

Step 1 This is a Wolf thought.

Step 2 My brain can't process Wolf thoughts properly

Step 3 Lord, your word says...(quote scripture verse)

Step 4 Lord, thank you for what you are doing...

Repeat this process as many times as you need to. Initially, you may feel that you have to do this recurrently, and in fact, you just might. Your brain is used to processing these thoughts and dwelling on them. This is a counter attack. The Word tells us to *"take captive every thought to make it obedient to Christ"* 2 Corinthians 10:5bNIV. It will take time to retrain your brain. Imagine if you were taught how to swing a golf club one way and then years later after swing your club that way, someone showed you a new way. It would take practice. It would take a while for you to do the new swing with ease. Appendix A will give you some scriptures to start with.

Strategy 3 – SEEK WISE COUNSEL

Seek out resources that understand what you are up against. Advice from sources that don't understand wolves will prove to be ineffective, since some tactics only work with "normal people". Wolves don't play by the same rules as others!

All the books included in my end notes are can provide a wealth of information. In addition, I strongly suggest finding a therapist who can support you in this process. If the therapist is trained to help you deal with either a controlling or narcissistic spouse, you are on the right track. You are far better off seeing a secular therapist trained in these two areas than a Christian therapist who isn't. Sadly, the church and Christians are often blinded by Wolves that are "dripping with practiced sincerity". If you have to see a secular therapist, make sure you have wise spiritual guidance coming from other places.

Strategy 4 – TURN THE TABLE WITH ADMIRATION

Next it is time to start turning the tables on the Wolf. He or she has begun to expect that you will react in certain ways to his or her behaviors. By nature, a Wolf tends to be very suspicious of others. It is crucial that the Wolf doesn't realize that you perceive them as such, meaning the Wolf should believe that you believe you see them as an innocent and harmless sheep. I have worked with many women who, against my advice, go home and say, "Honey, I know what's wrong with you." Recall the tale of Little Red Riding Hood? When Grandma identified her intruder as a Wolf, he ate her. Calling a Wolf, who is dressed like a sheep, is a very dangerous thing to do. Don't jump ahead of God on this one. God, who sheds light on truth, is the only one who knows a heart is ready to transform. Wolves cunningly pretend to be broken and contrite in an attempt to not be exposed. A true Wolf may also admit to being a Wolf if it helps them get what they want; however, they will then demand vengeance and hunt you down for exposing them.

So, how do you turn the tables? You become their number one fan. Wolves love the praise and worship of others! Because Wolves oftentimes have charming and engaging qualities, you can find ways to do this sincerely. Do you remember King Saul? He started out with a heart after God, but his self-absorption got the best of him. 1 Samuel 9:2 says "*...Saul, a most handsome young man. There was none finer – he literally stood head and shoulders above the crowd.*" Wolves are usually tons of fun to be around (as long as you aren't expecting anything from them). Compliment them on how much people enjoy spending time with them.

Wolves also appear to be very generous; however, their generosity has a selfish purpose. Either they mean for their benevolence to be publicized or they are attempting to captivate their prey through gestures of generosity. The reality is: a Wolf's motivation is not of a selfless nature. It is to make them look good. You can still compliment them on the positive difference their giving made in another person's life. Look for the truth amidst the web of confusion and deceit, and praise them!

One of your greatest strategies of defense is a Wolf's need for image protection. Lacking the ability to self-reflect, a Wolf creates a false persona and then thrives off the reflection he or she wants others to see. Therefore, a Wolf will dwell and prey wherever they receive admiration. But, if the Wolf is being fed "admiration", he/she is less likely to prey. The difference between a Wolf receiving admiration and being fed admiration is in the giver. Feeding a Wolf with admiration implies that the giver is intentionally taking care of the Wolf's need for admiration. Whereas, when a Wolf is seeking out admiration, oftentimes, the giver is unaware that they are in the presence of a Wolf.

I remember watching a reality show that portrays this strategy explicitly. The show revolves around the father—how great he is, how smart he is at making money, and how many woman admire him. He has no problem telling you how wonderful he is. He has never married the mother of his children, yet they have lived together for twenty plus years. She has mastered the art of feeding her Wolf with admiration. When she has a need, she either figures out how to meet it herself or she is very strategic in how she does it. In one episode, she wanted to have plastic surgery. Rather than asking her husband, she helped him to see how they could both benefit from keeping their younger look! They both ended up having plastic surgery together.

Strategy 5: LET GO OF THE EXPECTATIONS THAT A WOLF WILL MEET YOUR NEEDS

Remember, a Wolf will only be inclined to meet the needs of others if it is beneficial to them. The Wolf will meet expectations to trap their prey or maintain and manage their image. While the public may be led to admire the Wolf because of their adept role-playing abilities, few people, usually those near or subordinate to them, experience the Wolf's true colors.

One Wolf I encountered was gifted in helping people in crisis. Wherever a crisis could be found, the Wolf was consoling. This was his means of trapping vulnerable prey. In many instances, it was also a means of publicity for all his "good work". Upon meeting this particular Wolf, you may have found him charming, sincere, generous, and even empathetic; however, within a few months of interaction, his sharp teeth would start to show. In reality, he had a long trail of destruction in his past. The fruit he bore at home through his troubled children testified to his Wolfishness. His fruit he bore with his subordinates at work testified to his Wolfishness. However, to the public a different picture was painted. He was a master at clouding the trail of destruction that followed him—it was always someone else's fault. Christian ministries were lured by his smile, a smile "dripping with practiced sincerity." As he built his web, there was mass confusion and massive havoc. This was his cue to move on to a new flock of sheep. In some instances, the new flock was warned of his manipulation by a few courageous survivors, but the Wolf's charm led the sheep to ignore such warnings.

Consider this story of Saul in 1 Samuel 14. While winning a battle against the Philistine's, Saul's soldiers who had been drafted by the Philistine's and soldiers who had been hiding in the hills joined in. Do you know what Saul's response was after their victory? He cursed anyone who ate before he had vengeance on his enemies. HELLO? Can you imagine? After attaining victory, shouldn't he be giving the glory to God? Shouldn't he be thanking his loyal soldiers for fighting with such tenacity? Shouldn't he be thanking the men for their return? Shouldn't he be encouraging the troops? Shouldn't he be restoring them physically? Rather, Saul forbids them to eat until he has had vengeance on his enemy. His self-absorption and need for vengeance was more important than caring for those he was leading.

Interestingly, if you go back a few verses, Jonathan, Saul's son, had snuck over to the Philistine's side without his father noticing. And what was preoccupying the king? "*Meanwhile, Saul was taking it easy under the pomegranate tree at the threshing floor.*" (1 Samuel 14:2 MSG) Amidst the bashing and thrashing of war, Saul was enjoying a lovely afternoon picnic. Talk about self-absorption. On the other hand, Jonathan was trusting God, not his father the King.

"Jonathan said to his armor bearer, "Come on now, let's go across to these uncircumcised pagans. Maybe God will work for us. There's no rule that says God can only deliver by using a big army. No one can stop God from saving when he sets his mind to it." (1 Samuel 14:6 MSG)

In my opinion, Jonathan knew his dad was a Wolf. I think Jonathan had lived a life replete with needs unmet by his father. I also think Jonathan had learned that God was his true father and provider of all his needs. Jonathan realized his dad wouldn't think about the needs of the fatigued and starving soldiers. Do you know what Jonathan's response was to Saul's command to not eat? *"My father has imperiled the country. Just look how quickly my energy has returned since I ate a little of this honey! It would have been a lot better, believe me, if the soldiers had eaten their fill of whatever they took from the enemy. Who knows how much worse we could have whipped them?" (1 Samuel 14:29&30 MSG)*

Jonathan learned firsthand what it means to be as "cunning as a snake and as inoffensive as a dove" when amidst Wolves. Remember if you are married to a Wolf, don't expect them to meet your needs. If they are meeting needs, beware, because it is benefiting them in someway. Wolves don't meet the needs of sheep. Wolves eat sheep! If you are ready to release your expectations of how your needs should be met and put your trust in God, you will be saved from the Wolf! In your marriage, you will see other ways to having your needs met. Jonathan didn't expect his dad to lead Israel to victory; he knew it was God who would do that. This was only the beginning of Jonathan's wisdom: he knew to be available to God; he knew to ask for God's blessing; he knew Saul would not meet his needs; he knew not to wait on Saul but rely on God.

God is the provider of all your needs. Furthermore, God knows your needs better than you do! He knows your situation. He also knows the Wolf's next steps and how to counter that move. Seeking God and resting in His care of the situation is key. God's resources are abundant; He can meet your needs beyond what you imagine. God's provision isn't dependent on the Wolf's resources! Finally, like Jonathan, who crossed over enemy lines without his father's permission, you must be ready to act upon God's promises.

God oftentimes has us step out in faith. Remember the Israelites had to cross over the Jordan in to the Promised Land, the priests had to put the soles of their feet into the Jordan's water and then the river stopped. I have read somewhere that in order for this to have happened, God had to stop the river twenty miles upstream. He went before the people of Israel!

Strategy 6: DEFLATE AND RUN FOR SHELTER AS NEEDED

In general, don't battle with a Wolf—you usually won't win. Matthew 10:22 LB says, *"It isn't winning you are after it is survival, so be a survivor."* One of the most effective parenting techniques of a toddler is redirection, meaning getting them involved in something else, rather than saying "NO, you can't have that". The same principle applies to Wolves. When they start ranting, first try to redirect them. This is not a time to get caught in an argument with them. If their ranting progresses into a tantrum of "I want what I want when I want it," your next best alternative is to quietly excuse yourself (i.e. "Just a minute, I have to go to the bathroom.") Take this time to pray for wisdom and direction. Pray for God to protect you. Pray for God's peace. Psalms 91: 2-4 LB says, *"This I declare, that he alone is my refuge, my place of safety; he is my God, and I am trusting him. For he rescues you from every trap, and protects you from the fatal plague. He will shield you with his wings! They will shelter you. His faithful promises are your armor."* If the Wolf is still ranting after your bathroom break, you will need to give him or her a time-out. Wolf time-outs need to be strategically planned. You must make pre-arrangements with trusted friends. Ask a close friend if he or she is willing to keep a change of clothing for you (and your children) at their house. Also, ask them, should the situation arise, if you could stay overnight. If they are unable to accommodate you, ask them to still keep the bag at their house with money in it to pay for a hotel room. Next, ask them if they would be willing to be part of a phone "escape plan" for you. It is important to have an additional backup person or plan in case your first friend is unavailable. If you are so isolated that you don't have friends you can trust or your spouse has been physically abusive with you, it is imperative that you contact your local domestic violence shelter to help you create a safety plan.

Here are some ideas on creating escape plans.

Escape Plan 1:

If the Wolf is still attacking after you have tried redirecting him or her, it is time to prepare for a safe escape. When you go to the bathroom for your "time out," bring your cell phone with you. Call your safe person and ask them to call you back in five minutes to see if you are okay. If your safe person, doesn't answer, go to your backup person.

When you come out of the bathroom, assess the situation. If the Wolf is redirected by your absence, when your safe call comes, chat briefly and casually. But if the Wolf is still on the prowl, when your safe call comes in, say something like:

"Oh, my gosh! What happened? Are you okay? Don't worry, I will be there as soon as I can?"

Hang up the phone and calmly say to your spouse.

"My friend, ____________'s car broke down, and she has the kids with her (or some version of a believable reason that requires you to leave immediately). She isn't able to reach her husband, so I need to go help her. Honey, I know this issue is important to you, and I love you and want to work this out. I will be back as soon as I can." A plausible story will eliminate suspicion.

Leave the house. This bigger redirection and time-out should be enough to calm the Wolf down and distract him or her. Most likely the next time you see the Wolf, he or she will act as if nothing happened.

Escape Plan 2:

If your Wolf is too angry to let you leave the house, try this alternative: excuse yourself to go to the bathroom and call your safe person. Ask them to come to your house, preferably with their spouse, as soon as possible.

Take a deep breath, come out of the bathroom and continue to try to deflate and redirect your Wolf until the doorbell rings. Once your friends arrive, most wolves will drop their vicious behavior in order to maintain their image in front of others. Have your friends stay as long as they need too.

Escape Plan 3:

Find someone who your spouse respects and will also believe what is going on in your home. While you are in your time-out, in the bathroom, call them and ask them to call your spouse. The purpose is to divert the Wolf by getting him or her to do a social activity, like playing a game of racket ball. Usually a self-absorbed Wolf will be happy to do something they enjoy. Once again, when the Wolf comes home from playing racket ball, most likely he or she will act like nothing happened.

Escape Plan 4:

If, despite your best efforts and prayer, the Wolf is still on the attack, it's time to leave your house temporarily. Have your key readily available, and make your way to the door. After you leave, text your spouse a message, "Honey, I love you. I will be back when you have calmed down." Don't answer his or her persistent calls or text messages until you notice a change in the tone of messages he or she is leaving. If his or her tone hasn't calmed down by evening, it's time to go to your trusted friend, get your bag, and make arrangements for the evening. Wolves fear abandonment, and it is very possible they will move from anger to neediness, thus making it safe for you to come home.

If any of the following happens....Call 911! If you should ever be assaulted physically, this is imperative. Even if your spouse's job has negative consequences for this type of infraction, you still need to call. Don't ever let the consequences of his misbehavior stop you from protecting yourself. If your spouse threatens suicide, call 911, and a trained person will assess whether your spouse is suicidal or not. If your spouse ever threatens your life, call 911 and make sure you contact your local domestic crisis shelter.

If your child is ever abused physically, it is critical that you report it, and take your child to the doctor or emergency room immediately. Physicians are mandated reporters and are legally bound to report the incident.

Do not be afraid of taking these steps. In both of these instances, it is critical for you to take a stand. Sometimes systems fail, but in the majority of cases, they don't. I also suggest that you put your children in therapy, preferably, art or play therapy if your child is under twelve. Your kids need a safe place away from the chaos of the Wolf. Therapists are also mandated reporters, and over time, they should gain an accurate picture of what is happening at home.

Remember, save standing up to the Wolf for what really matters and when you feel God is leading you to stand up.

Strategy 7: BEWARE OF A WOLF'S TRICKS AND TEARS

Be wary of those times when the Wolf appears to make a desperate plea of repentance. I have seen and heard countless pleas with tears, some of which could have earned the Wolf an Academy Award. Remember, Wolves will do whatever they need to do to get their way.

Wolves are terrified of intimacy and also of abandonment. Their fears of intimacy and abandonment create a push and pull dynamic in a relationship. You will have those moments when you "couldn't feel closer" and those moments when you "couldn't feel more distant". When a Wolf feels you are pulling away, they will pursue you. When the Wolf feels you want too much from them, they will pull away. It will be important for you to learn to stand steady amidst the Wolf's pushing and pulling. A Wolf will only let go when you have served his or her purpose.

True change takes time! Amidst Wolves, you must always be on guard! Don't ever assume, in any of his or her brief "sheep like" moments, that he or she gets it. Remember, change takes time and hard work. You need to see a change in behavior, actions, and attitude for a long period, at least six months. Most Wolves cannot carry on a charade for longer than that. However, this isn't a magic number; I have heard of Wolves appearing to change their ways for as long as two years. It is possible, depending on the dynamics of his or her relationship, for a Wolf's true colors to stay hidden for years. This is especially true for Wolves who have finely crafted images of themselves. When life circumstance become difficult, their false image will crash and their true colors will be exposed.

Over the years, I have heard such sad stories of the vengeance of wolves. The great lengths a Wolf will go to in order to meet his or her needs or protect the carefully constructed façade of self never cease to amaze me. Recall how King Herod killed thousands of Jewish boys under the age of two, including his own son, in an attempt to extinguish the new born King. King Herod also put John the Baptist's head on a platter just to watch his daughter dance. Unless you want your head on a platter, it is imperative that you are "as cunning as a snake and as inoffensive as a dove".

Chapter V
How Did You End Up With a Wolf
Becoming the Sheep God Created You To Be

The irrefutable truth is that each of us has a God-given value that cannot be rescinded by the declarations of misguided humans. Somewhere along the way, you allowed a narcissistic human to become your final authority, not God.
Les Carter, Ph.D

When a sheep realizes they have married a self-absorbed Wolf, it is time to ask, "How did I end up marrying a wolf?" There isn't a simple answer to this question. The answer starts with the fact that your identity hasn't been defined by Christ! It has been defined by others. Certainly this is an issue we all face as we are transformed into His image, but for the sheep married to a wolf it goes back to his/her childhood.

Before I begin a chapter that could give everyone the idea that it is okay to bash or blame your parents, let me lay a foundation. It is important to be considerate of God's commandment to "Honor your parents" first! I believe the majority of parents, if asked, believe they did the best they could with what they had. However, we all have blind spots to our own self-absorption. King David was known "as a man after God's own heart." Yet, through his distractions and blind spots, his daughter Tamar was raped by her brother Absalom. (2nd Samuel 13:1-22) After the rape, David still didn't step up to the plate in the way he should have as a father for Tamar. If I were the family therapist to the King, I would have been appalled by his behavior and most likely beheaded for my work with Tamar.

There are several kinds of home environments that increase a person's vulnerability of marrying a self-absorbed

Wolf. The bottom line of all these environments is that they didn't produce sheep whose identities were formed by Christ; rather they were formed in their parents' identity.

The first home environment that makes a person vulnerable to marrying a wolf is where the dysfunction was easily seen. In a home where there was physical or sexual abuse, it is obvious that a child's emotional need weren't met. In a home where there is domestic violence, it is obvious that a child's need for security wasn't met. In a home where there is an addiction, it is obvious that there are times when a child's needs weren't met. In all these homes, the child was not encouraged to develop his or her own sense of identity, as it was a threat to the dysfunctional functioning of the family. Certainly, if you grew up in a home where there was an addiction or some form of physical or sexual abuse, you know you came from a dysfunctional family. There is a plethora of reading material to help you learn to overcome the difficulties you are now facing. A quality therapist can also help you put the pieces back together to gain an understanding of your behaviors from experiences in your childhood.

There is a second type of home environment that is much harder to identify, that makes a person vulnerable to marrying a Wolf -- the "ideal religious family". A religious home follows all the rules and everything appears to be in working order. In these homes, there doesn't appear to be a Wolf. Some of the most destructive Wolf homes are the ones that have the appearance of being the "perfect family". The incongruence between what friends and neighbors perceive to be versus the reality of what is really happening is so extreme that the child doesn't learn to trust his or her own impressions. Pressman and Pressman in *The Narcissistic Family[26]* refer to what they call the covertly narcissistic family. Children raised in this type of home have many of the symptoms of a child raised in an obviously dysfunctional family; however, there is no obvious evidence of dysfunction. *"There was no overt abuse; nobody drank or took drugs. The family actually functioned very well. Children were fed, were clothed, had birthday parties, took family trips, and graduated from good schools. The family looked normal, even on close inspection." (15)*

What do you think the home life of the Pharisees looked like? Do you think their homes were perceived as being solid? Do you think the children's emotional needs were considered in keeping all the "rules" the Pharisees had created? Do you think their children's "good behavior" was a reflection of the Pharisees or a reflection of who God wanted their children to be? Sound familiar?

I often wonder if amidst all our rules for the Christian family, we are ignoring or neglecting who God created our children to be. I wonder if we get so caught up helping them keep the "rules" that reflect what a good Christian looks like that we neglect who Christ is forming our children to be. If my child were roaming around the desert eating locusts and honey and proclaiming the good news of God's son, I might think she suffered from schizophrenia. If my child gave up her career as a successful fisherwoman to follow some radical dude who didn't even own a home or at least a rental agreement, I would believe she was in a cult. If that same dude was taking her off to hang out with tax collectors and prostitutes, I would be desperate to provide some kind of intervention. If my daughter carried her only child to the top of a mountain to sacrifice her son, I would call the police! If my daughter and her son had only enough flour and oil for one final meal, and she shared it with some guy named Elijah, who was running from Queen Jezebel because of an order for his death, I would be mortified.

In Erwin McManus' book, *The Barbarian Way[27]*, he describes this kind of passionate following of Christ. Yet, when it came to his own daughter, he had a hard time dealing with her dream to make a billion dollars, and then give it all away to the poor and needy, even if it meant she was homeless herself. He said, *"It took me a little while, but suddenly I saw it clearly. I was experiencing a barbarian invasion. Mariah's heart was beating to the rhythm of the heart of God. And her dreams were way too raw for me. I didn't see it initially, but I was trying to civilize her instead of unleashing the untamed faith within her. After all, I am her dad. It's okay if I live a life of irrational faith and breathtaking adventure. I want something different for her. I want her to have security and safety—you know, a predictable, boring, mundane life where I never have to worry about her again. In that moment I realized Mariah would have none of that. For her there is only one path. Even at twelve she has already committed to it. Be still my heart, but my daughter has chosen the barbarian way out of civilization."* (11 & 12)

Our desire for our children's safety and security may make us a model parent, but it would be self-absorbed in the sense that I would be trying to control my child's future, rather than trusting in the path that God was directing for her. My question is this: Were you raised in a home where Christ was your final authority or your parents? My next question: Are you raising your own children to see Christ as the final authority in their life or you?

According to Pressman and Pressman, *[28]"The parent system's ability—or, more accurately, inability—to focus on the needs of the child or children is the determining factor in defining a narcissistic family."* (19).

This illustrates what happens in the home of a child raised by a covert Narcissistic Wolf; the parent doesn't accept responsibility for meeting his or her own needs. Rather, the parent looks to the child to meet needs of the parents. In this process, the child does not develop a trust in his or her own feelings and opinions. The child's feelings become a source of discomfort as the parent doesn't allow or teach the child to express his or her feelings, nor does the parent validate the child's feelings. The child will typically respond in one of two ways; he or she will either rebel against meeting the parent's need or the child will comply. So, let me ask you a really difficult question. In a Christian home, where there are expectations of how we should "look". How is a compliant child perceived? How is the rebelling child perceived?

One client told me a story of her teenage daughter, Sarah, who had just come home from her dad's second wedding and realized that she had forgotten her makeup at her dad's. It should have been a simple solution, call the dad, and get the makeup sent. The situation was further complicated by the fact that Sarah and her mother were on their way to a conference with the school dean. With her mind anxious on the impending meeting, Sarah quickly phoned her dad to inquire about the make-up. The dad became infuriated by the hasty call. Julie, Sarah's mother, took the phone and tried to mollify the dad's rash anger. She attempted to explain that Sarah was stressed over the upcoming meeting with the dean and did not mean to offend him, yet the dad could not be calmed. Julie insisted that the dad only talk to Sarah after his anger had subsided, to which he replied, "How dare you prevent me from talking to my daughter when I want to." He called back, and Julie answered the phone and told him that Sarah couldn't talk as she was going into a meeting with the dean and that she would explain later. The dad was livid. After meeting with the dean, the mom called the dad to explain what was going on. The dad ranted at the mom for not letting him talk to his daughter when he wanted to. The mother continued to try and explain what was going on, but the dad refused to listen and continued to rage. The mother finally said to the dad, "I am going to hang up know and I will have Sarah call you after you have calmed down"

Consider what Sarah's emotional needs were. First, being a teenager, she was at a time where fitting in is fundamental to emotional development, hence the make-up. Next, she had just spent the weekend at her dad's wedding (remember, 2nd marriages aren't exactly most kids dream for their family). Third, she was on her way to meet the dean and was filled with emotion. What did Sarah need from her dad emotionally? Several things would have met Sarah's emotional needs: appreciation for having come to her dad's wedding, validation for how difficult it must have been, and concrete action towards finding the missing make-up. When the dad discovered there was a meeting with the dean, he should have expressed concern and let her know he wanted to hear about and how it turned out. Instead, the dad was focused on not being able to talk with his daughter when he wanted to. The dad was focused on how he felt disrespected by her quick phone call. Whose emotional need was taking precedent?

Children, like sheep, have two problems. First they aren't self-sufficient, so they need a shepherd or a parent to take care of them. This brings us to their second problem, children and sheep will follow the voice they recognize. The question becomes: whose voice is being followed and whose voice is the parent or shepherd following? The first voice we learn to recognize is our parents. Their influence in our life has a huge role in what voices we recognize and follow in the future. According to *Trapped in the Mirror*,[29] Elan Golomb says, *"A common problem for children of narcissists is that we do not know when to stop being mistreated. We do not even know when we are actually being mistreated since we accept suffering as a means to winning favor."*(152)

Therefore, if you were raised by a parent who was suffering from self-absorption, you are going to be drawn to voices of self-absorbed wolves. They are familiar to you. You have been trained to put forth valiant efforts while you are being mistreated. When God was trying to help you recognize your still small voice as a child, it was stifled in an attempt to survive.

We don't automatically recognize Jesus' voice as children. Do you remember Samuel as a child when he was still living with Eli (1 Samuel 3)? Samuel heard God's voice three times, the first two times he thought it was Eli and went running to him. The third time, Eli directed him and let him know if he heard the voice again, it was the Lord calling him. If a parent doesn't recognize his or her own voice in Christ, how can he or she lead the children to recognize God's voice?

This lack of awareness needs to be redefined and reshaped by Christ. Once you start looking to Christ in terms of defining you as a person rather than your spouse, you will begin to be able to see the mistreatment. This can be a very scary process. It goes against every thing you have been taught. The key is to remember that what you have been taught has been skewed by the voice that you were listening to.

I have met many a sheep who have believed that boundary setting was selfish. I have met many a sheep who thought saying "no" was sinful. I have met many a sheep who had a twisted sense of submission. They were easy prey for a self-absorbed Wolf to lead them into harms way.

In *Trapped In The Mirror[30],* the author, Elan Golumb, states the following about the effect of having a narcissistic parent; "*The extent to which they manifest problems specific to having a narcissistic parent depends upon the degree of severity of the parent's narcissism and the presence or absence of ameliorating influences in the child's life...One reason narcissistic homes can be so destructive is that the narcissists tend to be insular, having only a few close friends who are also narcissists, equally insensitive to the needs and feelings of children. Others drawn to a narcissist are themselves children of narcissists, too mesmerized by the replay of their early childhood relationship to take an autonomous position with regard to her children."* (25)

The first step to reclaiming yourself from the Wolf's grasp is to defining one's sense of self in Christ. God designed each of us to be unique. 1 Corinthians 12:12-26 says we aren't all feet. I have a very dear friend, Jayne, who claims that we are all narcissistic because we believe we are children of God. How true! As a child of God, we need to start by surrendering ourselves to Him and becoming who He created us to be. If we focus on becoming our best self without Christ, we are being formed in our own image rather than in Christ's image, and we run the risk of becoming self-absorbed in the process. God knows where our hurts are. God knows where our blind spots are. God knows where our imperfections are. God knows where we need work!

Kay Arthur in her book *A Silver Refined[31]* gives the following metaphor that is a beautiful description of trusting in God's refining process.

"Come, let me take you back to a Judean village in ancient days.

Inside a small, walled courtyard under a blue and blazing sky, there stands a refiner of metals. In his hands, gnarled with age, he is rolling and fingering a lump of ore. He watches the sun play on the streaks and veins of lead and other minerals running through this bit of rock chiseled from the bowels of the earth.

His experienced eye knows that, intermingled within this ore, there is silver.

He lays the ore on his worktable then builds his fire with care and wisdom of years. Soon the flames are rising in the pit situated against the courtyard's stone wall.

At the worktable he picks up his hammer and begins crushing the lump into smaller pieces.

He pauses occasionally to state at the fire, as if in study. From time to time he places more fuel upon the already-blazing coals and works his bellows until the flames are in a frenzy.

When the fire is right, he gathers the hammered bits of ore from the place of their crushing and lays them in a small, sturdy container of tempered pottery—his crucible.

He places the crucible in the fire and sits down beside it. A long day is before him, and this is where he will stay for as long as the metal is subject to the flames. Silver is too precious to be forsaken in the furnace, too valuable to be ruined through inattention.

Carefully he watches the fire. It must be maintained at exactly the right temperature for the right duration of time to accomplish its purpose. Slowly the ore softens. The silver, with its greater density and lower melting point, liquefies first, hissing and bubbling as oxygen is released. The still-solid impurities rise to the top of the molten metal. This is the dross, and the refiner skims it off.

Now he adds bits of charcoal inside the crucible. He

knows this will enhance the sheen of the silver. The carbon of the charcoal will keep the refined metal from reabsorbing oxygen from the air, which would only dull its finish." (1-3)

There is only one thing that will keep your self-absorption in check, and that is surrender and dependence to the ONE. There is great irony here. When you surrender and depend on Christ, you become more Christ-like. In this process, you are saying no to your way and yes to His way. You are saying no to your needs being met in your way. In this process, you are sacrificing your needs for the needs of another person. The way out of self-absorption is self-sacrifice! Hear me clearly though, it is not self-sacrifice that says, "and now you owe me because of my amazing self-sacrifice." It is self-sacrifice that says, "and you don't owe me anything." And, if the other person didn't recognize your self-sacrifice, you don't call notice to it! Remember, Matthew 6:19-22, tells us that we are storing up treasures for when we don't call attention to our self-sacrifice.

My dear friend, self-sacrifice through Christ is a bitter pill to swallow. It isn't easy by any means. It's scary. Everything within you will battle against it. The world's best counsel will battle against you. But, the sweet taste of transformation and the provision that God provides outweighs and overpowers the bitterness of the pill's initial taste.

Chapter VI
Surviving the Huffing and Puffing

If you're in a difficult place right now, perhaps you need to entrust the problem to the Lord and leave it to His hands awhile. He alone can storm the impregnable, devise the improbable, and perform the impossible. He alone can part the waters.
Robert Morgan

Once you begin to allow God to transform you, the self-absorbed Wolf you are married to will increase his or her huffing and puffing, but you are sheltered in His care. During this initial part of the transformation process, you will experience a lot of rough roads, you will also make mistakes along the way as you learn to finally recognize the voice God gave you and allow Him to transform you. I would like to provide you with a road map through the rough terrain of transformation.

The movie *Babe[32]* is a classic portrayal of trying to find your own voice. Babe is a pig who has been adopted by a gentle farmer who raises sheep. The farmer has two sheep dogs and Babe is cared for by the female sheep dog. She sees Babe's potential, as does the farmer; however, the male sheep dog is less than happy about a pig being a sheep dog. The farmer provides Babe with opportunities to develop his uniqueness and hidden talent. The female sheep dog gives Babe directions on how to manage the sheep in a way that has worked best for her. It turns out that sheep actually have a voice, and they give Babe a little wisdom in how to work with them best. They sheep also encourage Babe to be himself, rather than trying to be sheep dog.

Once Babe starts acting like the unique pig God gifted him to be, he was able to excel. In this movie, the male sheep dog was a typical self-absorbed Wolf that is stuck in his own ways because in his opinion, his way is not only the right way but also the only way of herding effectively. He thought himself superior to everyone and was unable to accept the differences and values of the other animals in the farmyard. The more Babe was encouraged to develop his own uniqueness, the more rage he encountered from the male sheep dog.

If you have been listening to and following the howl of a self-absorbed Wolf, make no mistake, they will not be happy when you start to hear your own voice and allow it to be refined into Christ's image. The Wolf becomes threatened because he is losing control as you begin to look toward God as your everything rather than your spouse.

Mary was just beginning her journey of understanding her own voice. Her husband wanted another family to move into their 1,400 square foot home while the other family was building a custom home. Inside Mary knew that this wasn't a wise thing to do. There were already major stressors on the marriage and having four adults and two children in a three bedroom home seemed like a recipe for disaster. Not realizing the depth of what she was truly up against, she expressed her opinion. Her husband said he had fasted and prayed and felt lead to have this other family move into their house with them. Not realizing she had her own voice, she submitted when the religious card was played. She also started counseling and the counselor had her read *Boundaries, Knowing When To Say Yes and When To Say No* by Henry Cloud and John Townsend. Now when I say Wolves will huff and puff to get their way and try and scare their spouse, just listen to what Mary's husband did when she started implementing some boundaries—he ripped the cover of the boundaries book to pieces. Sadly, the huffing and puffing temporarily worked and Mary became a compliant sheep again. Fortunately, a seed had been planted within her and she began to discover her own voice in other, more supportive places.

My dear friend, Mary was a lost sheep and if you are reading this book, either you are lost or someone very dear to you is lost. In Luke 15:3-7, Jesus gives us an illustration of a shepherd who leaves his herd to search relentlessly for the one who is lost. When we hear teachings of this scripture, we think of unsaved souls. What if Jesus also meant in this illustration to convey to us that He will relentlessly pursue us when scriptural truths have been misconstrued and are leading us astray? When a sheep has wandered away from the flock, it is in danger of a Wolf attack. When we don't recognize our Lord's voice, we are in danger of an attack by a self-absorbed Wolf. If you are in a self-absorbed Christian marriage, I truly believe that God is relentlessly pursuing to reveal His truth to you, not the one that has been defined to you by Wolves.

Surrender and develop your relationship with Christ

You can't do this alone! First, you need to make a commitment to getting to know Jesus and spending time with him daily! You can't get to know someone unless you invest personal one-on-one time with them. Set aside time in every day to pray and read. I would start with a prayer journal, although I would caution you on keeping this in a very safe place away from your spouse's ability to access it. A prayer journal is different from a regular journal, as you are writing down your conversation with God. You are also writing down your impressions from what you are reading from the Bible or other books. Speak from your heart. Tell God your feelings, frustrations, and concerns. He can handle them. Don't worry about doing it the right way, just start talking with Him.

During this one-on-one time, it is also imperative that you start reading your Bible. It is oftentimes how God will speak to you and reveal Himself to you. It will provide you with stories of other people's relationships with God. Matthew is a great place to start since it portrays many encounters with the Pharisees, and it will help you begin to discern the difference between societal and religious rules and Jesus' teachings. Try reading a chapter every day. In addition, I would suggest reading a chapter from Proverbs everyday.

Then document any fresh understandings you had in your prayer journal.

I would also suggest reading a spiritual growth book or devotional during your one-on-one time. Again, only read a few pages or a chapter a day and record anything that really spoke to you in your prayer journal. I cannot tell you how many times I have started my one-on-one with a concern and how all of my readings that morning aligned with what my concern was and gave me either peace or direction. In *The Imitation of Christ[33],* Thomas Kempis writes conversations between Christ and a discipline using scriptures, he says "*A book has but a single lesson but everyone who reads it does not profit from it in the same way, for I am the interior teacher or truth and the reader of men's hearts. I understand each one's thought and I encourage their actions, apportioning to each one as I see fit." (141)* I encourage you to go to go to a Christian bookstore and see where God leads you.

This one-on-one time is imperative to surviving the huffing and puffing. Life is difficult at times and it bombards us with constant distractions. The principles you will learn during this one-on-one time will carry over into other areas of your life as well.

As your day goes on and you experience interactions with your spouse, you may begin to feel beaten up. It is important to find ways to replenish yourself along the way. Learning to live in Christ's presence throughout the day sometimes seems impossible. Brother Lawrence[34], who lived during the 17th century, is renowned for his mastery of living in Christ's presence. He was in search of a way to meaningfully serve God, so he joined a Carmelite monastery in Paris but was ironically assigned to kitchen duty. Feeling a little insulted and confused, he grudgingly carried out his chores. God showed him that even the most menial tasks are holy when done for God's glory, and his attitude began to change. His radiance in his kitchen duty became so strong that people began seeking him out for spiritual growth. His thoughts were eventually published in a timeless classic entitled *The Practice of the*

Presence of God. God can and will use and transform you where you are, including in the midst of a self-absorbed Christian marriage.

There are a lot of resources available to help you stay in His presence. Listening to praise music is helpful for remembering who is really taking care of you. If you have iTunes, you can download great messages for free from the spirituality and religious section and listen to them on your computer or iPod. Memorizing scriptures that have a personal significance can continually help you to redirect your own negative thoughts or the voice of the wolf. For instance, when you are taunted with thoughts of hopelessness, Jeremiah 29:13 can be a powerful counter. *"I know the plans I have for you. They are plans for good and not for evil, to give you a future and a hope."*

Reframing the huffing and puffing into lessons

Reframing is a therapeutic technique that looks for the silver lining in the cloud. It is also biblical. Paul tells us in Philippians 4:8, to fix our thoughts on what is true, good, right, pure and lovely. Look for what you have that you can praise God for. You can even praise Him for the difficult times as God promises He is at work amidst it all (James 1:1-5, Romans 5:3-5).

When we start reframing our difficult circumstance, we experience a deeper faith. Do you remember that expression, "Be careful what you pray for"? Let me assume that this whole time of suffering you have been praying for a good marriage. Let me also assume that you have been praying to know God more. Consider the following quote by Larry Crabb in *Shattered Dreams[35],*

"When dreams shatter, we long to experience God's nearness in a way that dries our tears. Instead, deeper tears are released.

Perhaps that's why so few make any sustained effort to seek God with all their hearts, to discover how deeply they do in fact desire God. The discovery brings pain. We can get in touch with a profound desire that we have no power whatsoever to satisfy. We find ourselves at the mercy of One who could provide satisfaction but may not, a Person we cannot manipulate , an unresponsive God who keeps whispering, 'Later.' The start truth is a hard one: Discovering our desire for God introduces us to a whole new world of hurt. When we realize how badly we want him, He seeming disappears."

Now there is a RAW truth. What if that is true? What if the pain in your marriage is about something different than you thought?

Let me tell you a story about one of my dearest friends, Sandy. She has a great marriage! Her husband adores her! She is the sweetest and most joy-filled person I have ever met. When I was married to my first husband, I would have envied her. I would have also thought, how unfair.

Sandy and I met while we were on staff together at a church, a time when I was a single parent. We became friends and then became accountability partners. She was such a source of encouragement to me as I survived my single parent years. I remember Sandy telling me her prayer was to know God more (a dangerous prayer). Sometime after that, Sandy started having mysterious symptoms. For a whole year she kept getting sicker. Doctors couldn't figure out what was wrong. Amidst this struggle, she still could brighten anyone's day with her joyful, welcoming spirit.

Next, Sandy's job was taken away from her. She was able to go on the church's Cobra Plan, but after that, she had to go on a conversion policy, thereby paying over $2,000 a month for her insurance. Sandy eventually was diagnosed with Polymyosistis, a disease that deteriorates your muscles and has side effects like Type II diabetes, chronic pain, and depression.

Is there a silver lining in her story? Sandy can't divorce her illness. She has to live with constant chronic physical pain. Where is God amidst of her illness? Sandy's deepest desire is to be able to do ministry again. She spends her days praying and reading scriptures. When she can't sleep, she spends her nights praying and reading scriptures. Sandy prayed for me as I composed this book. She prayed for God to open doors to the publishing world. You know what, Sandy does have a ministry. She is a modern day saint in my eyes. I hope in sharing her story, you have the courage to continue on in your marriage and use Sandy's story as a reframe. Remember, she can't divorce her pain.

Larry Crabb[36], goes on to say, "*A profound encounter with pain brings us to make a choice. Either we change or we sink into bitterness, despair, or hedonism. Either we accept the fact that life is not all about us and how we feel now and what happens here, or we push back the pain by living for the satisfaction of lesser dreams that might come true."*(88)

Gary Thomas in *Authentic Faith*, says *The question is not whether we'll suffer, but how we'll suffer, and, just as important, how we'll respond to suffering."(68)*

If you have prayed a prayer to know God more, suffering will come your way. Christ suffered. If we are to be Christ-like, suffering will happen on your spiritual journey. Everyone's cross is different. Is your marriage your cross?

Other relational support systems

Another vital resource to surviving and transforming is relationships with others. Let me caution you, these close relationships should be with same-sex friends. The age old question that was asked in *When Harry Met Sally[37]*, where Meg Ryan and Billy Crystal are arguing about whether men and women can be friends or if sex always gets in the way, is still up for debate! When you are in a difficult marriage and you start sharing with someone of the opposite sex, you are becoming emotionally involved as they support you. You will begin to start wishing your spouse had the warm traits of you new friend, and you will soon be heading for trouble!

It is important to remember that you have a faulty tracking system that seeks out people who are self-absorbed; therefore, finding a professional counselor who can help you through this process is important. Counseling is a place where you can unload and share what you are experiencing and feeling. It is a place that can begin to understand what a healthy relationship looks like. It is a place that can encourage you to discover who God created you to be. Sadly, finding a solid counselor doesn't always happen on your first try. Start your process off with prayer and ask God to lead you to a therapist who can help you. Try getting the names of several therapists. Churches often keep lists of therapists that they recommend. Ask friends for personal recommendations of therapists. There are also websites that give you descriptions and qualifications of therapists. A good place to start is www.therapistlocator.net or www.goodtherapy.org

You also need to start opening up to trusted friends about what is going on at your house. Part of the power of a self-absorbed Wolf is in the perception that things are perfect. Share with friends who have a balance between validating what you are feeling and also being able to speak truth into your life. There is a fine line between being a friend who is grace-filled and speaking truth versus crossing the line into being one of Jobs "comforters". Friends won't always get the balance right, but a friendship over the course of time grows and changes as you grow and change.

I have been blessed with a 20 year friendship with my best friend Diane that started during the early years of my first marriage. She listened to me and accepted me, no matter what, during a time when I still didn't fully realize what was happening in my life. She also provided powerful statements of truth that always left me thinking. But as I grew and changed, she needed to grow and change. After my divorce, she said to me one time, "I have spent so many years with the Miserable Marj, that it is a difficult transition getting to know the Happy Marj." In this statement, she was telling me that she was willing to grow alongside me. One of my greatest joys has been watching the changes in her. I started out as a religious rule follower. She didn't grow up in church and deemed the rules too legalistic. Ironically, she was the one who knew her own voice, and she helped me learn how to hear my own voice. Then, as I surrendered my voice to Christ, she started seeing a difference in the religious rules and realized there was something personal there. I have watched her grow to see that God is someone who provides for you and cares deeply for you, and that He can be depended on. Healthy relationships support us, change us, and grow with us!

If you do not have any close friends, or you have had difficulty in relationships, there is a book called *Safe People*, by Henry Cloud and John Townsend that can guide you through the process of developing safe friendships. Support groups and recovery groups can also be healthy places. Remember: it is important to be discerning in all these relationships. Are they relationships that are encouraging you to develop your own voice and see who God has created you to be? If they are relationships that are telling you who you should be and what rules you should follow, beware, there may be a Wolf lurking!

The huffing and puffing will be disconcerting, but with developing your relationships with Christ and others, you will be supported as you travel this difficult road. It is a journey well worth the effort.

Chapter VII
Mirror, Mirror, On the Wall
Exposing Your Own Wolf-like Tendencies

Empty me of the selfishness inside.
Every vain ambition and the poison of my pride
and any foolish thing my heart holds too.
Empty me of me so I can be filled with you.
Chris Sligh

There are only a few places where we can see our own self-absorption. We don't notice our own self-absorption when we are out of the context of relationships. In the movie *About A Boy[38],* there are two main characters. Will is a single man who has been on his own for his whole adult life and he is quite proud of his "island living", as he finds relationships complicated. The complications Will's referring to are the requests that others make of us that required us to put another's needs before our own. The other character is a 13 year old boy, named Marcus. He lives in a single parent home with his mom who has major bouts of depression. After she attempts suicide Marcus realizes that we need more than one person in our life to have a healthy support system. He starts seeking Will out. Will has no idea how to respond. The remainder of the movie shows the challenges Will is faced with as he develops a caring relationship with Marcus but is confronting with his own self-absorption.

It is in the context of relationships that we are confronted with our tendencies toward self-absorption. Once you get past your pain, it will be easier for you to see your own Wolf-like tendencies of self-absorption. Hopefully you have started making several changes. You are learning to listen to your own voice. You are letting God transform you into His image of what your reflection of Christ looks like. You are depending on Him to meet your needs, not your spouse. You are beginning to understand the nature of the self-absorbed Wolf and no longer have expectations of your needs being met by your spouse. I want to go back to 1 Corinthians 13:4-7 and have you walk through it again, now that your perspective is different.

1. Love never gives up

Are you giving up on your marriage or are you starting to rest in God and His process now? Are you realizing that there is more to the process of a difficult marriage than suffering? Suffering is usually the greatest teacher for helping us to learn that love never gives up. Gary Thomas, in *Authentic Faith*, refers to a book written in the seventeenth century, *A Divine Cordial[39]*, by Thomas Watson. He believed that in prosperity, we are strangers to our self absorption. He believed that it was in afflictions that we were able to see the corruption of our hearts. Watson said that affliction was the "medicine that God uses to carry off our spiritual diseases." (68)

My friend, God's love isn't giving up on you during this difficult time. It is transforming you into the kind of spouse that God wants you to be! In my first marriage, I learned that God was the provider of all my needs. In my dating relationship, I learned what it meant to give and not get anything back. In my second marriage, I am reaping the benefits of the lessons I embraced.

2. Love cares more for others than for self

Have you started meeting your spouse's needs in a different way, with a different intention? I still vividly remember God beginning to transform me in this area. My ex-husband loved landscaping and gardening. I hated landscaping and gardening. I always felt like he cared more about the yard than me because that is where a huge amount of his spare time went. Sure, I could have gone out and helped him, but yuck! I grew up on a farm and hated outside work. I even went so far as to vow to myself that I would never marry a farmer. It was one place where I knew my own voice.

One day, I heard a very strong voice inside of me suggesting that I go out and help him with a load of bricks that had just been delivered. I knew it was God (I never would have come up with a thought like that). My initial response: *That is a crazy thought.* The voice from inside persisted to tell me to go help him. My next response was rebellion and justification, as I responded internally, *You have to be kidding, with all the unmet needs I have in this marriage, you want me to do something for him?* And God's response was, *Yes, but you are doing it for me.*

I have learned to love God's irony and sense of humor. I felt like my marriage was the land of Egypt and God was asking me to lay bricks. Thankfully, he wasn't asking me to make them. When we put our needs or unmet needs aside and care for others, we are really showing God how much we love him. Caring for others is an expression of loving others, and it speaks to the state of our own self-absorption.

3. Love doesn't want what it doesn't have

Are you still hoping to have the perfect relationship, or are you content with what God is providing you? Have you been able to look at your current situation and realize that God is providing you with what you need but in a different way than you anticipated? Are you seeing your unmet needs through a different lens? Is the focus removed from your spouse and looking toward God? Paul learned this lesson. In Philippians 4:11-13, he says, "*Not that I was ever in need, for I have learned how to get along happily whether I have much or little. I know how to live on almost nothing or with everything. I have learned the secret of contentment in every situation, whether it be a full stomach or hunger, plenty or want; for I can do everything God asks me to with the help of Christ who gives me the strength and power."* Remember, towards the end of his life, he literally was chained 24/7 to a Roman soldier. Indeed, your marriage may feel like you are chained to a Roman soldier, but you can learn the secret of contentment there, as Paul did!

4. Love doesn't strut

When God brings truth out, do you strut as if you were in the right? Are you filled with "I told you so"? Or, is your heart grateful for God's movement and work in the other person's life? Jesus interacted with Peter in a potential "I told you so" moment. In John 13:38, Jesus tells Peter he is going to deny Jesus three times. Peter insists that Jesus is wrong (talk about strutting). Of course, Peter denies Jesus three times. Jesus' next encounter with Peter in John 21 isn't, "I told you so". Rather, Jesus makes Peter breakfast and then three times tells him to feed his sheep. Love looks beyond the other's pride and when they fall, love humbly embraces and encourages them to move forward.

5. Doesn't have a swelled head

We are nothing without Christ. We have nothing without Christ. To think we can be separated from the person who created us to be is a mere illusion. If we believe that God was our maker as Psalms 139:13-16 says, then surely this is true. Christ-followers are called to love like 1 Corinthians 13 describes. How sad is it that many non-believers are better at a spirit of humility than Christians? Christians in their "rules" can easily become prideful. One of the things a Christian needs to battle is allowing righteous living to become a source of pride. It is God's grace that allows you to walk righteously!

In *Uprising: A Revolution of the* Soul[40], Erwin McManus says *"In Jesus we see that the power of God is unleashed to accomplish His greatest good when we are willing to walk in humility. The quest for honor is not where we pursue humility for greatness, but where we pursue the greatness of humility. The goal is not to know if you're humble, but to live as a servant, to give your life away for the good of others regardless of personal benefit or consequence."(62).*

Is it possible that your marriage may be teaching you how to live humbly?

6. *Doesn't force itself on others*

All of us have been guilty of forcing ourselves on others. Some of us are more tactful and covert, but nonetheless, we all do it. God created the world and gave man free will! God did not want to force Himself on us. He wanted us to have a choice of whether or not to be in a relationship with Him. I love the movie *Bruce Almighty[41].* Ironically, it contains some very sound theology. Bruce is authentically expressing to God how unhappy he is with his world. God relentlessly pursues Bruce until he recognizes Him, and then God gives Bruce access to His powers. Bruce uses the powers to get the promotion he thinks he deserves. He uses the powers to bring vengeance to those who he believes have wronged him. He decides to answer everyone's prayers with a yes, because there are too many for him to personally read and consider. He ends up losing Grace, his girlfriend because he is unable to see his own self-absorption and how it is causing her pain. Bruce does everything he can to force Grace back! He loves to be loved by her. Meanwhile, Grace has been praying for Bruce all along. Finally, she pleads to God to help her stop loving Bruce. Bruce is finally able to see what he has been doing and realizes he can't force love. He realizes that it is a more powerful love if it is chosen.

Love doesn't tell another person how they should behave! Love doesn't use scriptures of submission to lord over their spouse. Love lets a person be who God created them to be. Marriages so often have conflict over personality differences. One spouse is clean; the other is messy. One spouse is frugal; the other enjoys spending. One spouse is outgoing; the other is quiet.

Jon and Amy were on staff at the church where I worked. Amy had a calling to work with the elderly in church ministry. Amy was passionate about her calling. She pursued a master's in gerontology. Her ministry was thriving. Jon, on the other hand, was ready to do something different in ministry. Jon was my boss. He did his job. I had the utmost respect for him. He prayed. He waited on God. He stood by Amy in her calling. Eventually Jon's dad suffered from some serious health conditions, and Jon felt like he needed to be closer to home. Amy wanted to get her doctorate in gerontology. Jon started applying for ministry positions near his family. Jon waited on God's timing. He sacrificed his own desires and didn't force them on Amy. He trusted and respected what God was doing in Amy's ministry. Jon is a living example of what a husband does who loves God and respects the calling that God has placed on his wife's life.

Don't try to make your spouse something they aren't. We need to embrace the gift God gives each of us, even if we can't make sense of it!

7. Isn't always "me first,"

If we are loving, like Christ called us to love, we should be fighting for *you first*, but sadly in marriage, we are often fighting for *me first*. I have a standard intervention that I often use in couple's counseling to manage this one! So here is my intervention for every time a couple has a disagreement, no matter how petty or how large. If neither the husband nor the wife is able to be giving, or they are unable to find a compromise, I suggest they pray first and then flip a coin! You can only imagine the shock clients have at this suggestion. They are paying me good money, and I tell them to flip a coin. Hey, it is Biblical. Proverbs 18:18 LB says, *"A coin toss ends arguments and settles disputes between powerful opponents."* The majority of arguments that couples have aren't life or death—they are about preferences. When we start insisting on our way, we are being selfish! Here is what I know about probabilities: if you toss a coin you have a fifty-fifty shot of heads or tails. So, instead of the couple butting heads over their selfish stubbornness, the coin is the bad guy! The coin removes the control. If someone is unwilling to flip the coin, it is clear who is being *me first.*

8. Doesn't fly off the handle

If we are reacting in any unconstructive, unloving, or uncaring way, we are flying off the handle. We just fly off at varying degrees. Where and when we react is especially telling of the condition of our heart and where we need God's transformation. A heart that is transformed is able to step back from the situation. It is able to consider all persons involved and what their needs and concerns are, as well as what God's word has to say about the situation. The transformed heart is then able to act. It lives in the motto of "What would Jesus do?" However, that doesn't mean you react in anger that you justify your actions with the time that Jesus turned over the money changers tables in the temple. Remember, Jesus only did that once in his life.

9. Doesn't keep score of the sins of others,

I know from experience that living with a heart of forgiveness is probably one of the hardest things to do, especially in marriage. When you are in the midst of a relationship with a person like King Saul or King Herod, you are constantly forgiving. Can you imagine what it must have been like to forgive King Herod for killing your baby? One of my favorite books I recommend on forgiveness is by Robert Jeffress, *When Forgiveness Doesn't Make Sense.* Jeffress confronts the many challenges of forgiveness in those situations where harm has been damaging to the core of a person. One of the most challenging things for me is watching a Wolf get off the hook, while he or she continues to harm others. I can't even begin to understand God's accounting system, but I know His word repeatedly emphasized the importance and necessity of forgiveness. The Lord's Prayers says "forgive us our debts, as we forgive our debtors". In Matthew 18:22-35, Jesus tells the story of the man whose debts were forgiven by the king, and that same man proceeded to throw another person who owed him money in jail. The king then threw him in jail for not extending the grace he had been given. There is something very important in our journey of understanding forgiveness. If Christ was able to forgive His murderers and us, certainly part of the transforming process would include us having to forgive!

When you are living in a difficult marriage, especially one that involves a Wolf, you daily have opportunities to practice the art of forgiveness. Carol Kent, in her book *A New Kind of Normal* says, *"We're not happy about our circumstances. But we're not living in denial or bitterness either. We're just trying to be honest about how hard forgiveness is. It's difficult to understand and it's difficult to practice. We can set an intention to forgive, but it is a sticky process with many twists and turns, especially when we are still being hurt."[42]* Remember, forgiveness doesn't mean that we don't put boundaries in place when there are repeated patterns of sin.

10. Doesn't revel when others grovel,

I am always a little surprised by a spouse's reaction when the Wolf they are married to starts to transform. He or she usually does one of two things: either there is a judgmental "I told you so" or an exasperated "Now, he finally decides to get it when I am ready to move on." My friend, we never get to choose the timing of God's two-by-four that finally gets our spouse's attention. We are to respond in a Christ-like way whether we believe the other person deserves it or not. Your humility or your pride will be revealed in your response. If your spouse one day sees the light, it should be a day of rejoicing not reveling.

As a therapist, I constantly have the opportunity placed before me to revel. If I did, I would be a BAD therapist, and not in the sense of bad being good like it is in modern culture. Can you imagine wanting to go to someone who you have poured your heart out to and then when you screw up, they say, "I told you so". I think if I viewed my work in therapy as my own, instead of realizing that it is God working through me, I would say I told you so. I always say if I had become a counselor in my mid-twenties, I would have sucked. The journey God took me through my twenties and early thirties taught me invaluable lessons! I wouldn't trade one ounce of pain and suffering for where I am today; it makes me the person I am, and it has given me a spirit of compassion that I would never have had. I am only His vessel. When I give a cautionary statement in counseling, the Holy Spirit is the one who determines the how of the truth unfolding, not me.

11. Takes pleasure in the flowering of truth

When you start having your "ah-ha" moments, there is great joy! The flowering of truth brings about change. What a great metaphor! Think about it. Picture a rose bush with just green leaves and thorns (ouch). Picture a rose bud. Picture it slowly opening. Picture it growing into full bloom. What a beautiful sight! That is how we should look at truth unfolding. There are thorns along the way and we need to be careful. The reality is, we probably will get pricked and bleed. When trust starts coming out, it is usually painful. Trust me, the day I helped lay bricks, the thorns were not pleasant, but the truth that God started unveiling to me was a rose worth cherishing.

12. Puts up with anything,

What an unnerving scripture! I take great care and caution to not have you misinterpret this. Remember, an angel led Joseph and Mary to flee Bethlehem in the middle of the night before King Herod started slaying all the two year olds.

However, I am not talking about staying in a physically abusive relationship or risking your life.

Rob Bell, senior pastor from Mars Hill Church, in Grand Rapids, Michigan did a series called *Calling All Peacemakers[43]* which shed new insight for me in reference to verses that inferred putting up with anything. For instance, in Matthew 5:39, Jesus tells us to turn the other cheek. I have always taken that literally, meaning I would let the other person slap my left check. Guess what, that isn't what it means. In ancient Roman culture, the Israelites were occupied by the Romans. Everyday the Israelites encountered the rigid rule of the Romans. Jesus was telling them that He understood they were being humiliated and exploited. Sound familiar? Jesus provided the Israelites with an alternative.

In Hebrew culture, each hand had very specific purposes. Your right hand was considered clean. It was used for eating. The left hand was considered unclean and was used it to take care of your body. A slap in Roman culture was something a person of a higher position would do to a person of a lower position. A hit was something you would do to a person who was your equal. So, if you turned the other check after the slap, the person had to hit, rather than slap. When he turned the other cheek, he was blatantly saying "I am your equal". Jesus was telling them to not react in the same way the Romans were when He said to turn the other check. Turning the other check to a person in authority meant that he could not slap you again. If he did, he would be admitting that he was your equal. It sent a strong message against the power and violence. Indeed, love puts up with anything, but that doesn't mean that love doesn't stand up to wrong doing.

13. Trust God always,

Trusting God in good times is both easy and simple. Trusting God in difficult times is harder. Brennan Manning in *Ruthless Trust: The Ragamuffin's Path to God,* says,

"Unwavering trust is a rare and precious thing because

it often demands a degree of courage that borders on the heroic. When the shadow of Jesus' cross falls across our lives in the form of failure, rejection, abandonment, betrayal, unemployment, loneliness, depression, the loss of a loved one; when we are deaf to everything but the shriek of our own pain; when the world around us suddenly seems a hostile, menacing place—at those times we may cry out in anguish, 'How could a loving God permit this to happen?' At such moments the seeds of distrust are sown. It requires heroic courage to trust in the love of God no matter what happens to us."[44] (3&4)

God can be trusted in your marital discord. Trusting in God during the unknown is a far deeper trust then when you can see the path clearly laid out for you. During the unknown years of my single parenting, God provided me insight in the story of Peter walking on the water to Jesus (Matthew 14:22-33). As long as Peter kept his eyes on Jesus, he didn't sink. When he looked at the rough water and the storm clouds, he sank. In difficult times, as well as good times, our eyes need to be focused on Jesus. Regardless of what our circumstances are telling us, our eyes need to be on Jesus, otherwise we are swallowed by the tide of our trials.

14. *Always looks for the best,*

Finding the best in a Wolf or a situation that involves a Wolf can be difficult! It involves the technique of reframing that we already discussed. It is about taking a negative situation and finding the positive in it. It also gives us another opportunity to look at our own self-absorption. Dr. Les Carter in *Enough About You, Let's Talk About Me* says, *"Observing someone else's problems can prompt you to become honest about your own tendencies in the same direction. Knowing that we each have a self-absorbed child inside us, it is good to examine our emotions about behaviors routinely and see if we can detect selfishness."[45]* (41).

My husband, Mike, is an amazing man. He has a

heart that loves like 1 Corinthians 13. I have to work hard at not taking advantage of his kind and giving spirit. When it was time to take my daughter off to college, he offered to drive the 18 hour drive to take her belongings to college. He then suggested my daughter and I fly to her college so we didn't have to take the long road trip. Since he and I are both self-employed, this also meant taking several days off of work with no pay. He worked Saturdays throughout the summer to make up the financial difference. Never once did he complain. So, as I tell you the following story, keep in mind his generous heart that I was forgetting about.

One Christmas, we were trying to figure out how to put up tables for a dinner for fourteen people. I wanted to have the two tables set up separately, since my tablecloths were different reds. It would have also allowed a better flow of traffic in our minimal space. Mike, coming from a large Italian family who always had a long, never ending table, wanted the tables pushed together. So, sadly, we started butting heads. His way or my way. Did we flip a coin? Did we follow Proverbs 18:14 that says, *"It is hard to stop a quarrel once it starts, so don't let it begin."* No, we argued more. Finally, I gave in and we put the tables together. My first reaction was being upset at his stubbornness, which he later apologized for. The reality is that I was just as stubborn and selfish, and it took me a lot longer to see it! I was battling for the aesthetic look. He was battling for a family tradition. Mike was thinking of all the others at the table. I was thinking of the how it would best look. In afterthought, I should have surrendered before the fight began, especially since he is a constant source of giving to my preference. I should have remembered the best in him. Erwin McMannus, in *Uprising: A Revolution of the Soul,* says *"If only you could fool yourself as easily as you seem to fool everyone else. But at the end of the day, while everyone else gets to go ome, you can't escape the one place you can't stand. You're desperate to escape, but there's no way out, nowhere to run, nowhere to hid. You're stuck—with yourself... What do you do when the very thing that's suffocating you is the person you've become? What do you do when you can't stand the sight of yourself?"[46](19)* My own internal Wolf was lurking.

15. Never looks back

If you keep looking at the road behind you, you aren't going to be able to move forward. It is very easy in marriage to look backwards and provide a list of wrong doing. The scoreboard is always running. The artist Mary Englebright has a painting where a hobo is walking down a path, next to the hobo is another path that says "No Longer An Option". If we could make this a motto in our marriages, there are a lot of arguments that would never happen. The past would not be an option to bring up in arguments. However, I am not talking about ignoring destructive patterns and putting your head in the sand. But, we can easily get caught into our old patterns.

One of my favorite therapy theories is called Solution Focus. It helps the couple focus on when the problem isn't happening! The theory embraces something called the miracle question. *"If a miracle were to occur tonight while you slept, what would be different when you woke up?"* You would be amazed at how many solutions people can find. God says He will be a lamp onto our feet (Psalms 119:105). He was talking about moving forward!

16. But keeps going to the end.

God is the one who determines our ends. Marriage is more than a commitment; it is a covenant of three people: you, your spouse, and God. From the bottom of my heart, I understand the frustration and pain in these words. I also understand that God always makes a way! God released the Hebrew people from their captivity with Egypt! When they were trapped between mountains, the Red Sea, and the Egyptians, God made a way and opened the sea. *In Rules of the Red Sea[47]* by Robert Morgan, he says, *"In the Red Sea account, the Lord intended from the beginning to gain glory for*

Himself by snatching His people from the jaws of annihilation at the last moment. He never worried about the outcome, knowing He could provide an escape route at any time...Admittedly the Lord doesn't always deliver us from our problems in the way we want Him to. He does it His way, but in the long run His way is always best, and it always leads to worship." (25 & 26) My dear friend, rest in God's end, not your's. Psalms 36:5-7 LB says *"Your steadfast love, O Lord, is as great as all the heavens. Your faithfulness reaches beyond the clouds, Your justice is as solid as God's mountains. Your decisions are as full of wisdom as the oceans are with water. You are concerned for men and animals alike. How precious is your constant love, O God! All humanity takes refuge in the shadow of your wings."*

Chapter VIII
Wolves Eventually Get Exposed

Often the one who delights in evil is an ordinary, unassuming person who hides behind a façade of normalcy. Few people who are evil every appear evil, even after the evidence of their deceit, destructiveness, and hardness is exposed.
Dan B. Allender & Temper Longman III

Watching wolves get away with things is SO frustrating. It is even more frustrating when they continue to create havoc in others lives. Sadly, wolves are often in leadership positions. They give the appearance of being wonderful, but it is those closest to them, under their power, that know the other side of the Wolf. Wolves were in leadership in the Bible too: King Saul, King Herod, Pharaoh, the Pharisees, and the multitudes of evil Kings that Israel had. Oftentimes, it seems like God isn't doing anything, which can be very confusing. It is painful, and it can cause you to become angry and frustrated.

King David can provide valuable lessons in two of his life experiences. The first is from 1 Samuel 24, David is hiding in a cave from King Saul because Saul is hunting him down. Because King Saul was human he needed to relieve himself, meaning he had to go to the bathroom. He walked over to a cave and took care of business. Guess who was in the cave—David and his men. David had the perfect opportunity to kill Saul! David also knew once Saul was dead, he was going to be king. David also knew and trusted that God was in control.

David's men thought he should take advantage of the moment and kill the King. David actually snuck up behind the King and took part of his robe, but was then convicted that even though King Saul may be evil, he was indeed God's chosen king. After King Saul left the cave, David called down to him and let him know of the dangerous situation he had just left, and he let King Saul know that he understood that King Saul was God's chosen. Do you know how King Saul responded? Tears. He acknowledged that David was the better man because he repaid evil with good. He also asked God for a blessing on David and then acknowledged that David would be King. He asked David to spare his family when that time came, and David agreed. WOW! Talk about lessons in how to respond to evil. Trust God's timing of removing a Wolf's position. When the opportunity arises for you to remove them, wait on God. Acknowledge to the Wolf that your heart is to live and act in God's timing. Scripture doesn't tell us where King Saul's heart was when he died. God did remove him though and David became the new king of Israel.

David second experience occurred during his reign as King, a time in his life when he was displaying his own Wolf-like tendencies. In 2 Samuel 11 & 12, David couldn't sleep, so he went for a stroll on the roof. He saw a woman of unusual beauty taking a bath and he watched her. He then requested information regarding who she was. He learned her name, Bathsheba. He also learned that she was married to Uriah, one of his own soldiers. Let's stop for a second. What was up with David that he couldn't sleep? What was going on with David that he wasn't turning to God in his restlessness? And, most importantly, what was up with David watching a woman taking a bath, not to mention that her bathing was a part of the purification rites after her menstrual cycle?

Surely, when David learns that the woman is married, he would let it go. Nope, he goes a step further and has Bathsheba brought to him and sleeps with her. Turns out, she gets pregnant. Consequently, David sends for her husband to go home and sleep with her. Uriah is a dedicated and loyal soldier, so he sleeps outside the King's gate instead of sleeping with his wife. King David brings Uriah in and asks him why he didn't go home. Uriah responds to King David that the other men the army are camping out, and he would never be guilty of having comfort when they weren't also sharing that pleasure. King David then invites Uriah to dinner and gets him drunk. Uriah still doesn't go home and sleep with his wife, he sleeps at the palace gates. Let's pause again. Do you see how David is caught in self-absorption? Here is this man of God. He has killed giants. He has killed lions. He has trusted God. And, now that he has power, look at what he is doing. He's intentionally lusted. He has intentionally slept with a married woman. He has gotten her pregnant. And now, he is trying to manipulate the situation to his own gain. Talk about Wolf-like behavior!

Does King David stop here? No. Uriah has no idea that he is in the claws of a Wolf although he may be aware that King David is self-absorbed. Regardless, he is honoring his King, God's chosen. King David has Uriah sent to the battle fronts where it is almost ensured that he will be killed and indeed he is. King David allows Bathsheba grieving time and then brings her to the palace to be his wife. Talk about painting a picture of deception and making everything appear to look right. Now if that isn't Wolf behavior, I don't know what is.

Remember, David was known as a man after God's own heart. Jesus was going to be born out of the lineage of King David. In fact, Jesus was actually born out of the lineage of King David and Bathsheba's son, Solomon. God loved David so much that he sent Nathan to confront him. King David was initially defensive and resistant to this rebuke, but he eventually accepted Nathan's warning and because of this experience wrote Psalms 51, which is a powerful confession and request to be clean before God.

Being in relationship with a Wolf is intense. Only God knows a person's heart. Only God knows the person's capacity for change. I have learned that when I am working with individual married to self-absorbed Wolf or with a couple where one is a Wolf, I know that God knows the situation. His sovereignty allows me to know that change is possible;

however, it is conditioned on the person's willingness to change. Therapy becomes a series of tests or opportunities to turn toward God, repent, and change.

One of the most powerful stories of God transforming a Wolf is Tom and Kari. Kari came into my office broken. She had been married to Tom for fifteen years and just discovered that he was having an affair with someone at work. As she started sharing her story, it became evident to me that a Wolf was lurking in Tom. Kari's response surprised me. Yes, she was hurt and angry by Tom's behavior, but God had already been working in her heart to trust Him. Kari realized that her marriage had been an idol in her life. When she lost her idol, she was able to surrender fully to God.

Kari pressed into God's embrace. Tom continued to lie and cheat. Kari pressed into God's embrace. Tom left the marriage for the other woman. Kari pressed into God's embrace. Tom was given "tough love" by the men at the church. Kari pressed into God's embrace. Tom wanted to come back home and Kari let him. Kari pressed into God's embrace. Tom still continued his affair and got caught again. Kari pressed into God's embrace. Kari had biblical grounds for divorce. She continued to press into God's embrace.

During this time, I referred Kari to a book on Narcissism. After prayerful consideration and feeling led by God, Kari shared the book with Tom. I normally advise clients not to share this information with their spouse, as it can be used as a weapon against them. The book became Tom's Nathan. It exposed his Wolf-like tendencies. Tom was broken. The next morning, I got a call from Tom and Kari and Tom pleaded for me to let him come in to therapy. Tom came in my office broken. He told me he saw his own reflection in the book. I know from past experience that Wolves will admit to being Wolves when backed into a corner. I also know from past experience that Wolves can be great actors of repentance. And, I told Tom that. I also told Tom that if he wanted to change, it was going to be very, very difficult. I referred Tom out to counseling with a male counselor, and I started doing the couple's therapy.

Tom worked hard. He surrendered. He became accountable. Kari had to work hard. She had to rest in God and what He was doing, without assuming it meant Tom was really changing. Her marriage or hope for a solid marriage could never become an idol again. Kari also had to deal with tormenting thoughts and images in her head and forgive, and forgive, and forgive. Today, Kari and Tom have a strong marriage, but their first love is Jesus. Tom, like King David, surrendered and asked God to create a clean heart in him and to renew a right spirit (Psalms 51). Kari, like King David, waited on God for removal of the King, but rather than removing Tom, God transformed Tom's heart.

Wolves can change. It is one of God's modern day miracles! Remember, this transformation is conditional on the Wolf's willingness to change. Countless times in history God allowed the Israelites to live in bondage because of their evil ways. He was faithful to the remnant, the few who loved and trusted him.

The prophets Isaiah and Jeremiah are full of God's wisdom and how he handles wolves verses his remnant. They provide comfort in realizing He does see man's evil ways it and He will take care of it. In Jeremiah 23:1-4 LB, it is written,

"The Lord declares: I will send disaster upon the leaders of my people—the shepherds of my sheep—for they have destroyed and scattered the very ones they were to care for. Instead of leading my flock to safety, you have deserted them and driven them to destruction. And now I will pour out my judgment upon you for the evil you have done to them. And I will gather together the remnant of my flock from wherever I have sent them, and bring them back into their own fold, and they shall be fruitful and increase. And I will appoint responsible shepherd to care for them, and they shall not need to be afraid again; all of them shall be accounted for continually."

Jeremiah then tells of a vision he received about two baskets of figs in Chapter 24. One was fresh and ripe, while the other was spoiled and moldy.

"The good figs represent the exiles sent to Babylon. I have done it for their good. I will see that they are well treated and I will bring them back here again. I will help them and not hurt them; I will plant them and not pull them up. I will give them hearts that respond to me. They shall be my people and I will be their God, for they shall return to me with great joy." (verses 4-7LB)

Notice, God put them into exile for their own good. Look at what happens to the rotten figs.

"I will treat them like spoiled figs, too bad to use. I will make them repulsive to every nation of the earth, and they shall be mocked and taunted and cursed wherever I compel them to go. And I will send massacre and famine and disease among them until they are destroyed from the land of Israel, which I gave to them and to their fathers." (verses 8b-10)

God knows what is going on! God uses exile to purify us. Isaiah 28:7-9 LB says,

"Has God punished Israel as much as he has punished her enemies? No, for he has devastated her enemies, while he has punished Israel but a little, exiling her far from her own land as though blown away in a storm from the east. And why did God do it? It was to purge away her sins, to rid her of all her idols altars and her idols. They will never be worshipped again."

Is it possible that your difficult marriage is your exile? Is it possible that God is purging your idol of a good marriage so you will be rid of your idol once and for all? Is it possible that your spouse's self-absorption is their idol and God is using your difficult marriage to purge his or her idol for once and for all? God knows which basket your spouse is in. God knows if your spouse's fruit is going to be ripened or rotten. God knows if your fruit is going to be ripened or rotten. God loves His people. His desire is that none should perish. He will seek you relentlessly and he will seek your spouse relentlessly.

Chapter IX
Waiting On God's Time Clock
Wolves, Sheep, and Divorce

Letting go of our grip on predictable results and trusting God with our heart offering is one of the most challenging choices we make.
Carol Kent

We need to quit forcing things and enter the darkness of true liberty, where we give up self-efforts and allow God to interceded and draw us to our moment of readiness.
Sue Monk Kidd

As a therapist and as a Christian, I am hesitant to write a chapter on divorce. Divorce, being one of the most controversial topics addressed in the Bible, can be extremely divisive among religious groups. I realize that the Christian faith comprises numerous denominations, each possessing its own view on divorce. Even when discussed between scholars of the same faith and sect, debates concerning this issue oftentimes become heated.

It is easy to become frustrated with the variances of opinion on divorce. Many wonder why God didn't give us a handy rule of thumb, a simple test to diagnose whether or not divorce is acceptable in a situation. Wouldn't it be nice if the Bible outlined a "Divorce Checklist"? Adultery? Check. Non-believing spouse? Check. Irreconcilable differences? Check. Divorce? Check! Perhaps God foresaw that this sort of generalization would neither be conducive nor applicable to every marriage. As with most situations in life, there are special situations and circumstances, and God has refining to do in each situation. After years of witnessing Christian couples grapple with the decision of divorce and personally going through this in my first marriage, I would like to share with you what I have come to see. I want to use my words very carefully, and hopefully they won't be misinterpreted.

I am a divorced, Christian woman and a marriage and family therapist—how ironic is that? For some of you reading this book, that already is a problem. I hope that you have been able to hear my heart and its surrender to Christ thus far and will see that same surrender when it comes to divorce. For others, my being divorced brings comfort, you know I understand your pain and struggle. However, I would never want the fact that I am divorced to be taken as my being pro-divorce. I am not! If anything, my belief in marriage is now stronger. Divorce is painful. People get hurt. And, our children, who I know we love, bear a burden they should never have to deal with. Before you read any further, please take a moment to stop and ask God for His discernment while you read this chapter.

I have two guiding principles when working with someone who is considering divorce. The first is: do they have biblical grounds? If the answer is yes, then they have a green light to proceed with divorce, should they choose to do so. However, there is a second intersection they must pass through on the road to divorce. Even if they have biblical grounds, do they feel God is releasing them from the marriage? I call this the second green light. I will talk about it more in a little while.

The first question that may come to mind is, "how does one know if they have Biblical grounds for divorce?" In answering this critical question, let's start by analyzing the scriptural references to divorce. Jesus speaks of divorce in three of the four gospels. In Matthew 5:31 & 32 LB, Jesus says, *"The law of Moses says, 'If anyone wants to be rid of his wife, he can divorce her merely by giving her a letter of dismissal' But I say that a man who divorces his wife, except for fornication, causes her to commit adultery if she remarries again. And he who marries her commits adultery."* Most scholars and churches interpret this as if your spouse commits adultery, you have biblical grounds for divorce; however, others disagree. Pastor David Legge[48] discusses that the dissenting opinion is that the word fornication is referring to the betrothal period in Hebrew culture, meaning Joseph could have dismissed Mary because she was pregnant. Further evidence of this belief is the fact that Matthew was written to Jewish people while the other gospels were written to Gentiles. The other gospels, as you will see, don't have an exception clause to divorce.

Matthew 5:27-28LB provides further guidance: *"The laws of Moses said, 'You shall not commit adultery.' But I say: Anyone who even looks at a woman with lust in his eye has already committed adultery with her in his heart."* Many Christian scholars, pastors, and counselors will say that this verse can apply to pornography as grounds for divorce. I will be honest with you—I don't know the answer to that question. However, an answer is illuminated in the second green light, which we will come to later.

In Matthew 19:3 – 9LB, Jesus is confronted with one of the countless trick questions asked by the Pharisees. *"Some Pharisees came to interview him, and tried to trap him into saying something that would ruin him. 'Do you permit divorce?' they asked. 'Don't you read the Scriptures?' he replied. 'In them it is written that at the beginning God created man and woman, and that a man should leave his father and mother and be forever united to his wife. The two shall become one—no longer two, but one! And no man may divorce what God has jointed together.' 'The, why,' they asked, 'did Moses say a man may divorce his wife by merely writing her a letter of dismissal?' Jesus replied, 'Moses did that in recognition of your hard and evil hearts, but it was not what God had originally intended. And I will tell you this, that anyone who divorces his wife, except for fornication and marries another, commits adultery."* The Pharisees questioning Jesus represented two contradicting schools of thought. One believed that divorce was only permitted in cases involving adultery; the other allowed divorce under any circumstance, as long as the divorce was instigated by the husband since women were forbidden from divorcing their husbands.

In Mark 10:2-10, Jesus is once again confronted by the Pharisees on this polarizing subject. *"Some Pharisees came and asked him, 'Do you permit divorce?' Of course they were trying to trap him. 'What did Moses say about divorce?' Jesus asked them. 'He said it was all right,' they replied. 'He said that all a man has to do is write his wife a letter of dismissal.' 'And why did he say that?' Jesus asked. 'I'll tell you why—it was a concession to your hard hearted wickedness. But it certainly isn't God's way. For from the very first he made a man and woman to be joined together permanently in marriage, therefore a man is to leave his father and mother, and he and his wife are united so that they are no longer two, but one. And no man may separate what God has joined together.' Later, when he was alone with his disciples in the house, they brought up the subject again. He told them, 'When a man divorces his wife to marry someone else, he commits adultery against her. And if a wife divorces her husband and remarries, she, too, commits adultery."*

The final Gospel scripture concerning divorce is found in Luke 16:18; *"So, anyone who divorces his wife and marries someone else commits adultery, and anyone who marries a divorced woman commits adultery."* This scripture is found amidst a conversation between Jesus and the Pharisees about not being able to serve two masters, namely God and money. In this chapter, Jesus also tells the parable of the rich young man and Lazarus, which reveals the heart of the young man's devotion to his money. If you ask me, Jesus is making a point about the heart of man!

In 1 Corinthians, Paul also discusses divorce. Most Christian churches, pastors, and counselors will profess biblical grounds for divorce if you are married to an unbelieving spouse and he or she wants a divorce. In 1 Corinthians 7:15 Paul writes, *"But if the husband or wife who isn't a Christian is eager to leave, it is permitted. In such cases the Christian husband or wife should not insist that the other stay, for God wants his children to live in peace and harmony."* This scripture does not intend to say that a Christian spouse desiring divorce has Biblical permission. On the contrary, 1 Corinthians 7:13 & 14, explain this situation as an opportunity for the Christian spouse to witness to the unbelieving spouse. Furthermore, the verse clearly states that if the believing spouse wants out, it's not an option if the unbeliever wants him or her to stay.

I think it is important to step back and consider the culture of the time. Divorce was rampant, even among the Pharisees. The only act necessary to enable divorce was for the husband to provide his wife with a "bill of divorcement," and she would be forced to leave the house. The implementation of the "bill of divorcement" was a saving grace to the women of the time. Originally, when a husband no longer wanted one of his wives around he would simply "send her out," which was translated from the Hebrew word "shalach." This put the woman in a dilemma. She couldn't go back to her husband, neither could she find another husband because she was still technically married, and there was no way for a woman to live on her own in Hebrew culture. The man, on the other hand, could have as many wives as he wanted, so "sending her out" had no impact on him. The institution of the "bill of divorcement," which was the Hebrew translation for the word "Keriythuwth," allowed her to be single and remarry again.[49] She now had a means of provision. Obviously, there was a lot of confusion about divorce amongst the people and religious leaders. Somehow, I don't find it surprising that even today there is confusion among the people and religious leaders.

Recall how the Pharisees were trying to trap Jesus in Mark 10. While they were trying to back him into a corner, Jesus responded in a way that gave them an opportunity to reflect on their own hard hearts instead of undermining His words. With one group of religious leaders saying you can only divorce for adultery and the other group saying you can divorce for any reason, where is the truth? What if Jesus was saying, *"Hey if you are all going to play these silly word games, how about no divorce, that was God's original intent and you know it. Moses only allowed it because of man's hardness of heart."*

Is it possible that modern day Christian culture is guilty of the same thing? We line up the different schools of thought to determine when we have scriptural grounds for divorce. Then we proceed based on the answer we like best. The one that gives us Biblical justification for what we want. The answer is the same today as it was in Jesus' time, it comes down to man's heart.

As I stated previously, the first green light of divorce is Biblical grounds. Reflect on the verses provided above and see how they speak to your situation. The light may then turn green, but this does not mean that God intends for you to divorce your spouse. This brings us to the second green light. Has God given you release and peace? Are you letting God lead you through the processes of separation and divorce? Are you in a place of surrender to God and letting Him deal with your own self-absorption?

Sadly, one of the difficult types of marriage, where there are no scriptures directly saying it is acceptable to divorce, is when people are in abusive relationships. There is no first green light in this situation. However, abuse of any kind in a marriage is sinful! No where in the Bible is a person given justification to abuse someone: emotionally, spiritually, physically, or sexually. Abuse eats away at the very soul of a person and creates confusion about what is or isn't true, including God's truth. If you are in an abusive relationship, you need to surround yourself with God's truth about you and His amazing workmanship in how he created you.

The further a marriage suffers from self-absorption, the more abusive it becomes! Victimizing someone through words or actions, is just as abusive as someone abusing you. If our bodies are indeed a temple, and the Holy Spirit dwells within us (1 Corinthians 6:12-20), how can we not take a stand against abuse of any kind that is desecrating the temple?

Divorce is telling of the condition of man's heart. It reflects the self-absorption that leads up to it. The key is our HEART's alignment with God. Living by scripture is commendable, but NOT if we are using it to beat someone over the head with it. God is concerned with man's heart!!! Here is the deal with the first green light, do you have biblical grounds for divorce? If you line up ten different theologians, you are going to get ten different answers. I am not a theologian. I don't know Greek or Hebrew. What I do know is all sins are equal in God's eyes. Pride is just as sinful as adultery. Divorce is just as sinful as the sins of self-absorption that lead up to it.

This brings us to the second principle. Have you been released by God from the marriage? Do you have God's peace? Are you surrendered and walking with Him in your life and in the process of separation and divorce? Are you in a place of surrender to God and letting Him deal with your own self-absorption? Marriage was originally intended for companionship and teamwork. Within a few days of God's creating man and woman, self-absorption took over, and Adam and Eve ate the apple.

Let's look at an interaction Jesus has with a woman who was used to being abused by her own community and culture. In John 4:1-42, Jesus is walking through Samaria. At this time, the Samaritans were looked down on by the Israel elite. It was considered unclean to interact with them. Once again, we see Jesus hanging out where religious leaders would be mortified to even place their feet. To top it off, He runs into a woman and decides to ask her for a drink of water. This would have been seen as a huge sin. It gets worse. This woman has been married five times and is now living with a sixth man. To avoid being shamed and humiliated by the other Samaritan women, this woman was getting water alone, during the middle of the day. Seriously, this woman's self-esteem had to be in the pits. The religious rule of the day despised her, her ex-husbands despised her, and the women of her own village despised her.

Jesus doesn't condemn her. He doesn't lecture her on her five marriages. He talks to her heart. He only offers her living water, and he tells her he knows of her five marriages and current living situation. In John 4:14LB, He says, "*But the water I give them becomes a perpetual spring within them, watering them forever with eternal life.*"

She recognizes that Jesus must be a prophet of some sort, so she steps out on a limb and asks Him about the condition between the Jews and the Samaritans in reference to where to worship God. He goes on to say in verses 21-24, "*...The time is coming, ma'am, when we will no longer be concerned about whether to worship the Father here or in Jerusalem. For it's not where we worship that counts, but how we worship-is our worship spiritual and real? Do we have the Holy Spirit's help? For God is Spirit, and we must have His help to worship as we should. The Father wants this kind of worship from us. But you Samaritans know so little about Him, worshipping blindly, while we Jews know all about Him, for salvation comes to the world through the Jews.*" Jesus is telling her it isn't about the "rules," rather; it is about the heart! Do you know where the woman's hope is? She knows a Messiah is coming who will explain everything to her. In that moment, Jesus acknowledges to her that He is the long awaited Messiah.

So what does all this have to do with the second green light and divorce? Did you notice that Jesus only commented the facts to her? Did you notice that He didn't condemn her? Did you notice that He spoke to the condition of her heart, its emptiness and its loneliness? He knew this woman had been searching for solace and security in marriage, and it wasn't working. He offered her something different, Himself. The answer to her situation was the living water He had to offer her.

Your heart and its condition is what will illuminate or extinguish the second green light, and it also has to do with God's timing. I see far too many people trying to run ahead of God and find themselves in trouble. Leaving a Wolf is not something to do lightly or on your own. It needs to be done with wisdom, discernment, and God's leading. It is so important to stay below the Wolf's radar. Wolves have their own self-absorbed reasons for why they are still in the marriage. And, for some of them, the marriage isn't over until they say it is over. Quite honestly, the best way to leave a Narcissist is when they want to leave you. Usually, it is when they are having an affair. However, this is a very painful process, as oftentimes the spouse is completely unsuspecting. Marriages with Wolves have the capacity to appear like wonderful marriages for awhile, so when they come crashing in, it can be very shocking.

Amber and Daniel had sixteen years of perfect marriage. It was the ideal relationship that everyone looked up to. She was as in love after sixteen years as she had been when they met. She adored him. Amber had been having several difficulties at work. They had decided together that it was time for her to leave. On her last day of work, she realized she had forgotten some papers at home and had just enough time to get them before she had to be back to make a presentation. She walked in the house; something wasn't right. She walked down the hallway. Her son's bed was tussled, and her husband was in the laundry room wrapped in a towel. She walked into the guest bathroom and there was another woman. Daniel blamed Amber. He said cruel words to her about who she was and how it was all her fault. Amber was in shock.

What Amber didn't understand was that her perfect Christian marriage was only real to her. She had been married to a self-absorbed Wolf who had carefully crafted an illusion of being a perfect husband. What had finally cracked the Wolf was when Amber's attention was taken up by the problems at her work and she had less energy to focus on his every request. What Amber thought was true, wasn't. Amber realized that even though she thought she had loved God with her whole heart, she had placed a lot of her security in her wonderful marriage and wonderful husband. She had to rebuild her life. She didn't want a divorce. She told her husband that no matter what he had done, she would forgive him and still love him. She was still in love with the Daniel she had married. She didn't understand yet that Daniel was gone, that the Daniel she knew didn't exist. It had only been an illusion.

Amidst all her confusion, Amber pressed into her relationship with God. She lived in the moment, sought wise counsel, and waited on God. She prayed for God to soften her husband's heart. God gives people choices, and, her husband chose not to be married. Ironically, it wasn't long before her husband was serving as a youth pastor at another church, where everyone loved him as he served with "dripping sincerity."

There is one thing that is predictable with a self-absorbed Wolf, and that is their self-absorption. When a Wolf has a rigid set of rules that he or she lives by to give the impression of perfection, they may find themselves caught in their own trap. So instead of making a decision to get a divorce (because that would be wrong, and it would make them look bad), they make life at home miserable for those around them. Oftentimes, they are waiting for the other person to do the dirty work, so they can say, "my spouse left me." If this is your situation, God's timing in your second green light is going to be critical. There are things that God is doing during your waiting time. First, and foremost He is transforming you into His image. Second, God always stands on the side of marriage, so you will see Him diligently pursuing your spouse. Third, wait on God. Remember there were nine plagues before Pharaoh let the people of Israel go. When you are waiting, God is busy on your behalf!

Do you remember my free trip to Hawaii during my season of waiting and surrendering to God? It was that trip that spared my church ministry job when my husband and I ended up getting a divorce. The trip to Hawaii was very painful for me as it was filled with very difficult interactions with my husband, but most of these situations were witnessed by the other couple. The husband even flew to visit my husband after the vacation to confront him on what he saw. I waited on God for another one and a half years after that vacation, as I knew I wasn't spiritually released from the marriage. I learned to rest in God and press into Him.

During that time, God relocated me to another city, with my husband's blessing. God arranged for my husband to be at home one day and a phone call came from one of the pastors at the church verifying that indeed my husband was supportive of the move. In the fall, six months later our daughter started school in the new city. My husband still hadn't looked for a job, nor had he put the house up for sale. On one of his visits, I asked him, "What are we going to do?" He responded with, "I am not moving here." I said, "So, are we going to continue to commute?" He said, "No, that won't work." I said, "Are we talking about divorce then?" He said, "Yes, let's do that." Within one hour, we reached our own divorce settlement and filed without an attorney.

Next I had to let my church know that I was getting divorced. I shared my version of the story, but I also told them that they could contact the couple we had gone to Hawaii with if they wanted an outside perspective on what had happened. The church did contact the husband, who had been my husband's friend, and he shared what he had seen in Hawaii. God spared my job! And, he took me to Hawaii to do it!

I only know my heart to the extent that God has revealed it to me. He knows my heart fully. I don't know your heart. You only know your heart to the extent God has revealed it to you. He knows your heart. He is the finally judge on divorce and whether you have biblical grounds or not. Remember man's interpretation is limited by man's level of his revealed heart by God! The key is your heart's surrender to God!

My dear friend it is His timing, His way, and His leading that you must depend on. Divorce will not always be the answer. Sometimes God has things He is teaching you. Sometimes God is working out circumstances for the future. Sometimes God is doing things in your spouse's heart that you are unaware of. Wait in His sovereignty and care.

Chapter X
Safe Guards To Not Being Tricked Again

This chapter is dedicated to Greg, may you never be tricked again!

Maybe the blessing is the wound. Jacob limps now.
The man who stood and walked so well on his own two feet now walks wounded. The man who has lived crooked his entire life now literally walks crooked, but maybe he's beginning for the first time to walk straight.
This scar in his flesh, this twist in his bone, perpetually reminds Jacob of his dependence.
Every step is now a jog of the memory, a physical insignia that this is the way; walk ye in it.
Mark Buchanan

I wish I could give you a guarantee on this chapter. The truth is, not getting involved with another self-absorbed Wolf is like asking for a guarantee that your next spouse won't get cancer. Would you want a guarantee that you are marrying someone who will never have cancer? We all would. The best we can do is look at one's predisposition to cancer and what research has shown us about the prevention of cancer. It is the same with marrying a Wolf. Nina Brown in her book, *Children of the Self-Absorbed[50]* says,

"It is almost impossible for a therapist or anyone else to identify these aspects in someone as characteristic of destructive narcissistic pattern (DNP) until they've spent some time with the person. It is only over time and with consensual validation by other people who've experienced similar things with the person that one can arrive at the conclusion that the person is indeed a destructive narcissist."(16)

Wolf behavior is exposed over time; however, if you know predispositions and behavior patterns to look out for, you can minimize your chances of dating or marrying another self-absorbed Wolf. Remember we all have tendencies towards self-absorption. So, be careful to not see a Wolf in every corner. On the other hand, I believe the Wolf population is on the rise in our society that embraces "me first," so tread carefully.

The beginning of a relationship with a Wolf isn't the same as the end of a relationship with a Wolf, so I want to give you some signs to look for. If several of these red flags are present, my best advice is to RUN! The goal is to have a healthy relationship with a healthy person, not to hook up with another self-absorbed Wolf.

Healing Time and Knowing the Real Truth of Yourself

I really am not trying to bash this over your head, but you need TIME after coming out of a relationship with a Wolf. I cannot make this point strongly enough. I have seen far too many people, including myself, jump back into a relationship in an attempt to try to know they are still desired and move past the pain. This is a huge mistake! There are two main reasons for it. First, you need to figure out who you are again. Second, wolves prey on people who are coming out of relationships. And, if you have children, they need time to recover from the loss of their family and adjust to their new families. During this time, they need your attention.

If you have just come out of a relationship with a self-absorbed Wolf, you have a lot of work to do. The Wolf has filled your head and heart with false messages about yourself. They have projected their junk all over you, meaning that all their insecurities and things they didn't want to take ownership of are wrapped up into your self-worth. You have baggage you are carrying around that isn't yours! Wolves don't like to take blame, so they blame you. Wolves don't want to be responsible for decisions, so they often back you into a corner. Wolves like to be in control, so they manipulate. As a result your emotional processing system and beliefs about yourself are all confused. It literally takes time for your brain's emotional processing system to recover!

In the movie the *"Lord of The Rings: The Return of the King,"* [51]Frodo enters a cave with a spider. The spider casts a web around Frodo and entraps him in a cocoon, so he can't escape. Frodo needs the help of his friend Sam to rescue him from the Spider. You actually can watch both these scenes on *You Tube*, if you don't have a spider phobia. If you have been in a relationship with a Wolf, your emotions and beliefs about yourself are still wrapped up like Frodo was in the spider's web. You need to be unraveled. It takes time.

Picture a file cabinet. Your experiences, good and bad, with the Wolf were filed away and had meanings prescribed to them as they were happening. Because relationships with Wolves rarely have adequate closure, your file cabinet literally got dumped on the floor, and you need to take time out to re-file and give new meanings to events and words. Throughout the relationship with the Wolf you thought certain things were true, like you actually believed you had found the ideal relationship. All the events and words the Wolf said to you during this wonderful time need to be re-filed and given different meanings. What they said and did was more about capturing their prey, rather than it being about you. All the events and words of the Wolf said to you during the difficult times need to be re-filed and given different meanings. What they said and did was about rewriting their story of finding the perfect mate. Since they couldn't be responsible for making the wrong choice of an ideal mate, you have to become the problem.

In *The Narcissistic Lover[52]*, Cynthia Zayn and Kevin Dibble describe what happens, *"Since the Narcissist (N) follows no ethical guidelines, he/she does not know how to fight fairly. Victims of N's have learned the hard way that any of their weaknesses or vulnerabilities could be fair game for attack. It is emotionally dangerous for a partner or child to be exposed to the poison of an N's rage, especially over time. Since it is not rationally connected to anything the victim said or did, it is difficult to make sense of an N's anger. The confusion of the victim is a critical strand in the web of the N spins to trap the unaware and vulnerable. The N is a master at manipulation and knows the methods to use in order to effectively convince his/her victims that it was 'their fault' and that the N's narcissistic rage was justified." (86)*

Part of what happens when you have been involved with a Wolf is that they have told you who you are. It is more important for you to figure out who you are. What do you like? What do you want out of life? Who did Christ uniquely create you to be? Do you know?

I understand that you really just want to move forward in life. I also understand that someone saying wonderful things to you feels healing. But, be careful! A healthy person knows someone needs time to heal after a relationship ends. If a person is in a healthy place, they would never date someone just coming out of a relationship. If you had open heart surgery, would you run a marathon the day after, the week after, the month after? Before you run a marathon you build up to it, you get your body in shape. You train. Hopefully, you are hearing the seriousness of taking time to emotionally heal! You have just had heart surgery by getting divorced. The best thing you can do for yourself is hang out with friends who are of the same sex.

Your kids also need time to heal. They have just suffered a major loss. Children don't understand the adult reasons for divorce, and many times it isn't age appropriate to tell them details. My daughter Amanda said it best after her dad and I divorced, "Mom, I understand the divorce was good for you, but it wasn't for me." Her safe world, of a mom and a dad, was gone. She needed time to adjust to realize her new world would also be safe. I truly regret the energy I put into dating after my divorce. It should have been going toward her.

It is normal to want to hang out with people of the opposite sex. In fact, input from the opposite sex gives you a completely different perspective on situations. During your time of vulnerability, it is important that you do it in the context of strongly defined boundaries. Wolves have been known to prey by only being "friends," but their underlying motivation is still trying to find the ideal spouse. Being a part of a single parents' group can be very healing. Everyone there can relate to the difficulties of being a single parent and you can find support. However, keep your safety in numbers and don't spend time along with the opposite sex for awhile.

Another way to have input from the opposite sex in your life would be through your relationships with other couples. I had two very dear couple friends who always invited me to holidays and over for dinner. However, your time should always be spent with both the husband and wife. If you are doing lunch alone with the spouse of the opposite sex, you are heading for trouble.

If you are seeing a pastor of the opposite sex, the church should have strong boundaries around the relationship. Either the church will have a policy of no counseling the opposite sex, or they will have a policy of a limited number of pastoral counseling sessions. If those guidelines aren't in place, there is the possibility of trouble.

One relationship that should have safe boundaries with the opposite sex is a professional therapist. All licensed professionals have a code of ethics and legislative statues that make it unethical and illegal for them to become sexually involved with clients. Sadly, this isn't a fool-proof method, so be careful. The main reason therapist lose their licenses is because they get involved sexually with clients of the opposite sex.

Finally, people always want to know, *"how much time are we talking about?"* One ministry that provides recovery for people coming out of relationships is called Divorce Care. They recommend for every four years that you were married you should not date for a year. When I tell clients this, I get one of two responses. Either they say they are never going to be involved again, or they say they can't wait that long. In either case, the answer is unhealthy and coming from a place of pain! At minimum, I tell clients to not get involved with the opposite sex for six months after the divorce. You shouldn't be dating while you are still separated, because you are still married by law. I know some divorces take a long time; consider it God's protection from getting involved with another self-absorbed Wolf.

Take Time for God

I am assuming by now that you have realized that your marriage or the Wolf in your life has been idol. Exodus 20:1-4MSG makes it very clear that we are to not put anything else above God. *"God spoke all these words: I am God, your God, who brought you out of the land of Egypt, out of a life of slavery. No other gods, only me. No carved gods of any size, shape, or form of anything whatever, whether of things that fly or walk or swim. Don't bow down to them and don't serve them because I am God, your God, and I'm a most jealous God, punishing the children for any sins their parents pass on to them to the third, and yes, even to the fourth generations of those who hate me. But I'm unswervingly loyal to the thousands who love me and keep my commandments."* In Deuteronomy 6:4, we are called to love God with all our heart, soul, and mind. My question is: have you given God time yet to develop a relationship with Him? I know that you are well on your way. Your marriage to the Wolf can be likened to the Israelite's bondage in Egypt. God released the Israelites in His time from Egypt, and then they wandered in the desert for 40 years! During those years they learned to depend on Him in a different way. They had many hard lessons to learn before they were ready for the Promised Land. God provided manna for them daily! He told them when to stay and when to move. He knew they were used to the rule of Pharaoh. Pharaoh's rule was one of self-absorption, not of love. Pharaoh's rule wasn't even logical. God knew Pharaoh had a self-absorbed Wolf heart, and He knew that Pharaoh wasn't going to release the

Israelites without a fight. So, God played chess. In Exodus 5, God has Moses and Aaron request that Pharaoh let the Hebrew nation be allowed to go for a three day religious feast where they could worship God. Pharaoh not only says no, but he takes away the straw that the Israelites used to make brick, while still demanding they produce the same amount of bricks. Talk about a narcissistic rage! God knew what He had to do to unravel the rule of a self-absorbed Wolf, and the time in the desert was just the place to do it.

My dear friend, you need time in the desert to learn God's provision and care. There are lessons you couldn't learn during your time of bondage in a Wolf marriage. It is in the desert where you learn your vulnerability to false idols and longings to go back to Egypt. It is in the desert where you learn how much you grumble. But, it is also in the desert where you learn of His faithful provision. Don't miss out on what He has for you during your time in the desert!

Stepping Into the Jordon and Practicing What You Have Learned

Once you have finished your time in the desert, it is time to cross the Jordan into the Promised Land. Starting to date again can be a very scary thing. Remember the Promised Land was occupied by other nations that Israel had to conquer. Chances are you will go on a few dates with wolves before you meet another sheep. Hopefully, your Wolf radar is working and you will be able to spot them in a short period of time.

The movie, *About a Boy[53]*, powerfully portrays how attractive single parents are to self-absorbed people. Hugh Grant plays a character named Will. Will describes himself as a bloody bloker, who is superficial and an island. He needs no one else. However, he likes dating women for short periods of time, but even they are all too high maintenance for him. He gets set up on a blind date with a woman, who happens to be a single parent. When she tells Will she has a child, he thinks one thing, he doesn't like kids, and says another thing, he likes kids. Through the experience Will realizes the advantages to dating a single parent. He sees her as a lonely woman. He sees her as a woman who has been neglected, and he can easily be a good guy. She is preoccupied with raising her child, so it takes less work to date her. He plays with her kid, and she quickly falls for that. And, because she is lonely, she easily soaks up his kind words and easily goes to bed with him. Eventually he gets bored, as there is no cable at her house. When he goes to break up with her, she breaks up with him first. She says Will is the nicest guy she has ever dated, but she isn't ready for a serious relationship. Will has found his new pasture to prey in. He tracks down a single parents support group and pretends to be a single parent to get dates. He lies and makes up a pretend child and a pretend ex-wife. He buys a car seat and crumbles food in it to make it look used. The hunt is on.

I am not telling you this story to scare you. I want you to realize your vulnerability. We were made to live in community, not isolation. Being a single parent is a tough and lonely job. You are so busy with work and caring for your kids that I am sure you have little time for yourself. A simple gesture of dinner and a movie, where someone says nice things to you, can feel like you have died and gone to heaven. Pay attention and make sure this person really is capable of being there.

Too Good To Be True

At the beginning of a relationship with most wolves it feels like you have found "happily ever after." Remember the old saying *"if something is too good to be true, it probably is."* Such is the case with a Wolf. Wolves are always on a hunt to find the ideal partner. So, when they find someone new, that person starts off as their ideal partner.

In *Narcissistic Lovers[54]*, by Cynthia Zayn and Kevin Dibble, they say, *"At the onset of each new relationship, the*

Narcissist believes 'this could be it.' When she tells her partner he is the perfect fit or the best lover she has ever had, she really believes it is true. She wants so badly to be done with her tiresome journey and settle into 'happily ever after' that she makes herself believe she has finally arrived at the destination. Her disappointing past relationships, as far back as her childhood, are what motivates her to continue her quest for ideal love."(67)

What makes the Wolf's words so believable is that the Wolf believes with great conviction and passion what they are saying. The self-absorbed Wolf is in the process of rewriting his or her script of the ideal partner and you are being written into their script. At the beginning of many relationships with wolves there is a euphoric quality. Euphoria isn't love. It is a chemical reaction in your body, and Wolves are capable of casting a spell. If you are being told that this is the perfect relationship—beware! There is no such thing as the perfect relationship. If you are feeling like no one has ever known you better or understood you more perfectly—beware! It takes time for someone to know you, not magic.

Preying for Food

Wolves don't have their own food supply, so they steal from other people's food supplies. Narcissists have been compared to vampires, meaning they live off the blood supply of another rather than their own. Since a self-absorbed Wolf doesn't have a real self, they are in constant need of affirming their false self. In order to do this they stay very busy in an effort to avoid their real self. Usually their relationships are superficial. If they have a long term relationship, it is because they are getting food from the relationship.

At the beginning of a relationship, a Wolf is preying and trying to trap you. Be careful of gifts. Zayn and Dibble[55] say, "*When a Narcissist (N) gives a gift, you can bet there is something in it for her/him. An N will be the first to tell people about the money she/he spent on someone. N's feel the need to come across as altruistic people with generous hearts." (91)* I remember having dinner with a very dear cousin and his new girlfriend who was a doctor. My Wolf radar went up instantly when she started telling us a story of how she had spent a holiday with a dying patient and had taken him and his wife to a fancy restaurant. She also managed to speak several languages to the waiters during the course of the meal. From that moment, my radar was on, and over the course of time, her fangs were revealed. Sadly, it was only after she had managed to suck much of the life out of my cousin. Sadly, trying to rescue him was impossible, as the spell had already been cast. If I had tried to verbalize what I was seeing, I know how she would have spun my words. Indeed, later she tried to convince my cousin that I was a control freak and that he was too easily swayed by my opinion. Thankfully, he knew from experience that this wasn't true and continued to see me as a trusted person in his life.

In Erwin MacManus' book, *Uprising*, he akins a Wolf to a Tyrannosaurus rex, he says,

"Unfortunately, sometimes Rex is a picture of the most dysfunctional of human relationships. We see people as existing for our benefit. We are so desperate for friendship, so longing for love, that every time someone risks getting close to use, we consume him or her. We are so busy devouring that person's kindness that we are virtually oblivious to our lack of contribution. We don't even consider taking time to feed or nourish the other person. Pardon the phrase, but we become emotional leeches. We attach ourselves to the hearts of unsuspecting and compassionate individuals who hope to help us get better. We suck them dry of every ounce of emotional reserve until they are emaciated beyond the point of recognition. After they've gone from grape to raisin, we detach and look for our next victim. Just before we leave, to make sure we leave no good deed unpunished, we pronounce this judgment on them:'You told me you'd be there for me when I needed you. You let me down. You're just like everyone else.'

When you are a victim of this scenario, those final words are the crippling blow. Gasping for breath, you watch them walk away and quickly attach themselves to another unsuspecting caregiver. You would warn them except for one thing—you're free—and better them than you." [56](144-145)

Dance of the Wolf

A Wolf has a very predictable dance. Preying and spell casting are both steps in their routine. Distancing is also a part of their dance. Step one is to woo you. Usually because of your own pain, your reaction to this step is caution. This will increase the Wolf's wooing, until you surrender to their spell. The next step in the dance of the Wolf is bliss. There is a season of euphoria. The unsuspecting partner gets so caught up into the movement, that they don't notice the Wolf disappearing off the dance floor. When the partner opens their eyes, they are on the dance floor alone. In *Narcissistic Lovers*, this part of the dance is described as follows,

"The fear of abandonment which we spoke of earlier causes the Narcissist to secure his relationship by charming or convincing his partner that she herself is 'the one'. Once she buys into his ardent affirmations, she commits herself to the relationship and to him. The N's fear of commitment causes him to back away at this state. The hunt, the chase, and the manipulation are 'highs' for the N. The possibility that someone as special as his partner could want him is what drives him to gain her possession. Once he has her, however, he convinces himself that she must be flawed to want someone like him and begins to notice things about her that weren't as obvious in the beginning of the relationship. However, when something goes wrong, the relationship is no longer 'ideal' to the N. Once it is flawed. The relationship loses its value to him."[57](100)

However, the relationship is still not done at this point. Oftentimes, the unsuspecting dance partner will begin to pursue the self-absorbed Wolf in the hopes of regaining the fairy tale romance. In the process of pursuing the Wolf, the partner will usually provide words of worship and admiration of what an amazing partner he or she was. The Wolf will usually resist at this point as he or she isn't hungry. They will see the attempts of the dance partner as desperation, sometimes even referring to them as stalkers. Eventually, the dance partner will leave to regain a sense of self dignity. Guess what, a Wolf will get hungry again and he will attempt to go back to his last food source to see if there is anything left. And, the dance begins again.

If you are beginning to date again and you experience this dance...RUN! A Wolf won't prey where he or she isn't getting any food. If you aren't available, they will go elsewhere.

Creating a Safe Hedge

In Proverbs 4:23 NIV it says, *"Above all else, guard your heart. For it is the wellspring of life."* My dear friend, there are several things that guard your heart. It includes: you, your relationship with God, your knowledge and wisdom, the application of knowledge and wisdom, and the counsel of many. Proverbs 15:22 LB says, *"Plans go wrong with too few counselors; many counselors bring success."* One of your greatest safety nets is going to be those people in your life who truly care about you, believe in who you are, and respect you. Give these people permission to speak into your dating life. Let them meet the person you are dating! Ask for their feedback. Do they see any red flags? Talk with them about things that happen in the dating relationship that you aren't sure about. Learning to trust your own intuition is important; however, the reality is that your radar system still needs some fine tuning. It's tracking system needs to be rewired. The other reality is that when a Wolf decides to capture prey, even the wisest of people can be fooled. Those close to you are better able to spot inconsistencies because they aren't being charmed by the Wolf. Remember, God tells us there is safety in wise counsel.

Mark, a counselor friend of mine told me this truth about myself one morning before I had drank enough caffeine to hear it. I don't remember the context, I just remember his words. "Marj, you have an emotional radar system to emotionally unavailable men." OUCH! My response was "Really?" I have always considered him to be a wise counselor, so I decided to ponder his comment. Certainly, he was correct that my first husband had been emotionally unavailable. Obviously, there was some issue with the guy I had dated after my divorce, I just hadn't figured it out yet. That same night, I went to see one of my best friends, Kim. Her husband, Doug, was playing in a band. In walked this really good looking guy who went up to Doug and started chatting with him. I asked Kim who he was, but she didn't know. Later, I went up to Doug and said, "Hey, how come you never introduced me to that guy." Doug's reply was that the guy was stilling grieving over the loss of his wife who had recently died. Mark's words that had been spoken to me earlier in the day rang like clear bells! Out of a crowd of many men, I had been attracted to the one that was emotionally unavailable. Talk about a radar system that needed to be rewired! A part of rewiring your emotional tracking system is getting input from those who know you and value you. They can see things in the people you are considering dating that you can't.

My dear friend, cherish this season of difficulty that you are in. God has so much He wants to reveal in you and heal in you! Let Him! Trust Him! Rest in Him! In closing, I want to share the words to a song called *I Will Never Be* by Darlene Zschech. They were words that provided me with comfort and hope as I escaped my vulnerability to my own wolf-like tendencies and my vulnerability of being prey to self-absorbed wolves.

I will never be the same again
I can never return I've closed the door
I will walk the path I'll run the race
And I will never be the same again

Fall like fire, soak like rain
Flow like mighty water
Again and again
Sweep away the darkness burn away the chaff
And let the flame
Burn to glory your name
There are higher heights there are deep seas
Whatever You need to do Lord do in me
The glory of God fills my life
And I will never be the same again

My prayer for you dear friend, is indeed, that you will never be the same again and that your life will glorify His name.

Epilogue

When I was getting releases of information from one of my former clients to share her story, she asked me to please share the story of my daughter as hope to other single parents. During my daughter's senior year, Amanda was chosen to have a write up about her in a local magazine. The article was called "A Step Above The Rest". My client had seen the story and called to congratulate me and tell me how it has provided her with hope. Hope against the disheartening statistics that are so often quoted against children of divorce and single parenting.

As a parent, I of course love the opportunity to brag about my daughter's success. Her story is still being written, but she is off to a great start. I couldn't be prouder. She is off at college now and starting her own life. I am so excited about her future and the plans God has for her. She is kind. She is generous. She is caring of others. She is an amazing leader. She has integrity. She has a great sense of humor. She's intelligent. She's a quality person!

During her high school years, she made great choices! She chose to love Jesus! She chose quality friends. She chose to study and earned straight A's. She was a Valedictorian. She was diligent in goals she set for herself. She chose to be a leader in her community. She chose to remain sexually pure. She chose to stay away from alcohol and drugs. She chose to go to church and be an active part of the youth group. She chose to go on a mission trip and help with the clean up after Hurricane Katrina.

Surrounding our children with positive influences as single parents is critical! There were so many adults who took Amanda under their protective wings. I owe a debt of gratitude to each and every one of them who was a positive influence in her life. I also owe a debt of gratitude to those who took me under their wings and provided support and encouragement to me through all the difficult times of single parenting. A single parent can't do it alone. They need the help and support of others. And most of all, I am so grateful for God's provision and care!

Children also need access to both their parents (in most cases). They need their mom and their dad. They deserve to not hear their mom and dad talk negatively about the other. Amanda's dad and I tried, as best as we both could, to continue to do what was best for her, despite our differences. I am grateful for his faithfulness in providing Amanda consistent child support that afforded her many opportunities that I would have had a hard time managing as a single parent.

During Amanda's senior year, another one of my client's asked me how my daughter viewed the divorce and effects on her. So, I asked her. Her response will give you hope! You will see wisdom that only comes from having gone through a difficult time. Amanda's response was, "There were good things and bad things. But, I have learned that in the bad things, I was able to learn lessons I wouldn't have otherwise learned."

In writing this book, Amanda provided editing every step of the way. I wanted to take care in my words and try to be respectful of her father. I knew if she was reading, I would take greater care. Following is a poem that evolved out of the writing of this book. It started with the story shared at the beginning of my book. Next my creative actress and comedian friend, Jayne, took liberties of adding some creativity. Then Amanda transferred it into a poem.

The Good Christian Girl

Once upon a time there was a good little girl...

She listened to her parents. She listened to her teachers.
She listened to God, and she listened to her preachers.
She tried to follow all the rules and avoid trouble with boys.
With all these expectations, she became confused by the noise.
In situations, she strived to do every right thing,
Because she feared what the opposite would bring.

She read and studied her Bible every day,
From a righteous path, she tried not to stray.
She prayed *The Lord's Prayer* and lived what she was taught,
Life carried on like this, and she never gave it a thought.
The good little girl became a good young woman at a good Christian college.
She then studied and pondered, gaining good Christian knowledge.
And as if it were all in accord with a heavenly plan,
She even met and married the right and perfect man.

She thought if she did all the right things, the Lord would help her avert disaster. She thought she and her prince would live happily ever after...

But the good Christian girl never learned to listen to her own small voice,
How would she learn that God had given her a choice?

The good little girl grew up to be a good Christian wife.
In marriage, she followed the rules to minimize strife.
She went to church every Sunday; she read marriage books.
She sacrificed for him and took care of her looks.
Inside she was sad and lonely, though her marriage looked ideal.
How did she end up here, it all seemed so surreal.
Deep inside, her still small voice started talking,
But it was a very negative voice, so she resisted its knocking.
It pointed out all she didn't have. It pointed out all she was doing.
This voice was persistent; did it know what it was stewing?
This little voice scared the good Christian wife.
It made her realize she wasn't living a happily ever after life.

The good Christian wife started listening to her voice,
Even though it scared her, it was the right choice.

The good Christian wife was now in a bind.
The rules weren't working. Had she been blind?
Doing the right thing just wasn't working out,
She began to look at her marriage through eyes filled with doubt.
She considered divorce, but it didn't follow the rules.
Perhaps, she thought, God didn't give her the right tools.
She began to wonder how God could let this happen at all.
None of it made sense, how could He set her up for this terrible fall?

Meanwhile the good Christian wife became a good Christian mother,
And was learning to listen to her small voice for the well-being of another.
She was learning to listen to her small voice in other relationships as well,
This brought about prosper, it was easy to tell.
Maybe, she questioned, happily ever after wasn't the goal,
Maybe, she decided, it had something more to do with her soul.

Things were looking up, but the little voice inside her still doubted her marriage,
Was her husband not her prince after all, only a man disguised in a carriage?

She knew it was important to do the right things, but her motives were changing. She was learning how to give without receiving; this took a lot of life re-arranging. Then one night, after she had been backed into yet another wall,
A small, yet powerful, voice said, "You can depend on me to meet your needs one and ALL".
In an instant, she knew it was HIS voice that spoke in the dark.
His words brought her light, they ignited a spark.
The more she rested in HIM to meet her needs,
The more she started to hear HIS voice amidst her pleas.
By confronting the scariness of her own small voice,
She had discovered the sovereignty of HIS voice, by choice.

She realized that HE had been there the whole way.
HE had been guiding her path, day by day.
She realized that having a good marriage had become an idol,
She realized focusing on and following HIM was vital.
She remembered HE had made her; He wanted her to know who HE created her to be.
She had forgotten the faith and reliance of the good little girl you see.
It was in knowing herself that she began to understand,
Learning what it meant to be transformed into Christ's image by His own hand. She had not lost by gaining her reflection in Him,
The pain of the past was beginning to dim.
Her once upon a time had become a real story,
A tale of HIS transformation, sovereignty, and glory.

By Amanda Buchholz, Marj Castronova, & Jayne Post

APPENDIX A
Scripture References for Countering

Negative Thoughts

Step 1 **Lord, that is a Wolf thought.**

Step 2 **and my brain can't process Wolf thoughts**

properly

Step 3 **Lord, your word says**....*Let not your heart be*

troubled. You are trusting God, now trust me.

Step 4 **Lord thank you for what you are doing**...*to*

teach me to trust you.

Here are some other scriptures that may be helpful.

Let not your heart be troubled. You are trusting God, now trust in me. John 14:1

I am leaving you with a gift-peace of mind and heart! And the peace I give isn't fragile like the peace the world gives. So don't be troubled or afraid. John 14:27

Jesus replied, Every plan not planted by my Father shall be rooted up, so ignore them. Matthew 15:13

And we know that all that happens to us is working for our good if we love God and are fitting into his plans. Romans 8:28

That out of his glorious, unlimited resource he will give you the mighty inner strengthening of his Holy Spirit. And I pray that Christ will be more and more at home in your hearts, living within you as you trust in him. May your roots go down deep into the soil of God's marvelous love...Ephesians 3:16&17

Don't worry about anything; instead pray about everything; tell God your needs and don't forget to thank him for his answers. Philippians 4:6

...Fix your thoughts on what is true and god and right. Think about things that are pure and lovely, and dwell on the fine, good things in others. Think about all you can praise God for and be glad about it. Philippians 4:8

Marj Buchholz-Castronova, M.S. is a licensed marriage and family therapist. In addition, she is an Approved Supervisor through the AAMFT (Association of Marriage and Family Therapy) and supervises Interns and Students at two large congregations in Las Vegas. Marj also is an Adjunct Faculty member at Lincoln Christian University's Henderson, Nevada campus and is working on her doctorate in Marriage and Family Therapy at Loma Linda University. Marj and her husband make their home in Henderson, Nevada.

To schedule Marj for speaking engagements contact selfabsorbedwolf@gmail.com

Join the facebook fan page of Wolf: Self-Absorbed Christian Marriage.

References

Introduction Quotes to Each Chapter

Chapter 1
The Message
by Eugene H. Peterson

Chapter 2
When The Game is Over It All Goes Back In The Box
by John Ortberg

Bold Love
by DanB Allender & Temper Longman, III

Chapter 3
The Importance of Being Foolish
How to Think Link Jesus
by Brennan Manning

Chapter 4
People of the Lie
by M. Scott Peck

Chapter 5
Enough About You, Let's Talk About Me
by Les Carter, Ph.D

Chapter 6
The Rules of The Red Sea
Robert Morgan

Chapter 7
Empty Me (song)
Chris Sligh

Chapter 8
Bold Love
by Dan B Allender & Temper Longman, III

Chapter 9
A New Kind of Norman
by Carol Kent

When the Heart Waits
by Sue Monk Kind

Chapter 10
Your God's Too Safe
Mark Buchanan

Scriptures Quotes from

The Message
by Eugene H. Peterson
Navpress, 2002
Colorado Springs, CO

The Living Bible
Tyndale

End Notes

CHAPTER 1

[1] Jacob and Wilhelm Grimm, *Little Red Cap.*

[2] Joseph Jacobs, *English Fairy Tails* (London: David Nutt, 1998) no. 14pp.

[3] Jon Scieszka, *The True Story of the Three Little Pigs!* (Viking Press, 1989).

CHAPTER 2

[4] Beth Moore, *When Godly People Do Ungodly Things* (Nashville, Tennessee: Broadman & Holman, 2002), 43.

[5] C.S. Lewis, *The Screwtape Letters,* ed. HarperCollins (New York, NY: HarperCollins, 2001), 12.

[6] Neil Clark Warren, *Date or Soul Mate: How to Know if Someone is Worth Pursuing in Two Dates or Less,* (Nashville, TN: Thomas Nelson, 2005)

[7] Brennan Manning, *The Importance of Being Foolish: How to Think Like Jesus,* (New York: NY: Harper Collins, 2005), 65 & 66

CHAPTER 3

[8] Patricia Evans, *The Verbally Abusive Relationship,* Halbrook, MA: Adams Media Corporation, 1992)

[9] Max Lucado, *A Love Worth Giving*, (Nashville, TN: W Publishing Group, 2002), 7

[10] National Education Empowerment Foundation, 2006

[11] George R. Back & Ronald M. Deutsch, *Stop! You're Driving Me Crazy,* (New York, NY: G.P. Putnam's Sons, 1980)

[12] Bartels & Zeki, University College London

[13] Elan Golumb, *Trapped in the Mirror*, (New York, NY: William Morrow and Company, 1992), 155

[14] James L. Brook, *Spanglish*

[15] Patricia Evans, *The Verbally Abusive Relationship Relationship* (Halbrook, MA: Adams Media Corporation, 1992), 23

[16] Gary Ross, *Pleasantville*

[17] Patricia Evans, *The Verbally Abusive Relationship Relationship* (Halbrook, MA: Adam Media Corporation, 1992), 39 & 40

[18] Charles R. Swindoll, *Fascinating Stories of Forgotten Lives,* (Nashville, TN: W Publishing Group, 2005). 131-151.

[19] Dan Allender & Tremper Longman III, *Bold Love,* (Colorado Springs, CO: Navigators, 1992) 257

[20] DSM IV, Ed.4, American Psychiatric Association, 1994,

[21] Patricia Evans, *The Verbally Abusive Relationship Relationship* (Halbrook, Massachusetts: Adams Media Corporation, 1992)

[22] John Ortberg, *When the Game is Over It All Goes Back in The Box,* (Grand Rapids, MI: Zondervan), *238-240*

[23] 24 Patricia Evans, *The Verbally Abusive Relationship, Relationship* (Halbrook, Massachusetts: Adams Media Corporation, 1992), 91

[24] Charles R.Swindoll, *Fascinating Stories of Forgotten Lives,* (Nashville, TN: W Publishing Group, 2005). 107 - 108

CHAPTER 4

[25] Charles R. Swindoll, Jesus, (Nashville, TN: Thomas Nelson, 2008).

CHAPTER 5

[26] Stephanie Donaldson-Pressman and Robert M. Pressman, *The Narcissistic Family,* (San Francisco, CA: Jossey-Bass, 1994) 15

[27] Erwin McManus, *The Barbarian Way,* (Nashville, TN: Thomas Nelson, 2005), 11 & 12

[28] Stephanie Donaldson-Pressman and Robert M. Pressman, *The Narcissistic Family,* (San Francisco, CA: Jossey-Bass, 1994) 19

[29] Elan Golumb, *Trapped In The Mirror,* (New York, NY: William Morrow and Company, 1992) 152

[30] Elan Golumb, *Trapped In the Mirror,* (New York, NY: William Morrow and Company, 1992), 25.

[31] Kay Arthur, *A Silver Refined,* (Colorado Springs, CO: Waterbrook Press, 1997), 1-3

[32] Chris Noonan, Dick King-Smith, George Miller, ***Babe***

[33] Thomas Kempis, *Imitation of Christ,* (New York: NY: Vintage Books, 1984) *141*

[34] Brother Lawrence, *The Practice of the Presence of God* (Oxford, England: Oneworld Publications, 1993) First published: 1692

[35] Larry Crab, *Shattered Dreams,* (Colorado Springs, CO: Waterbrook Press, 2001), 88

[36] Larry Crab, *Shattered Dreams,* (Colorado Springs, CO: Waterbrook Press, 2001), 88

[37] Nora Ephron, ***When Harry Met Sally***

[38] Chris Weitz, Paul Weitz, Nick Hornby, Peter Hedge, *About A Boy*

[39] Cited in Gary L. Thomas, *Authentic Faith* (Grand Rapids, MI: Zondervan, 2002), 68

[40] Erwin McManus, *Uprising of the Soul,* (Nashville, TN: Thomas Nelson, 2003), 62

[41] Steve Koen, Mark O'Keefe, Steve Oedekerk, ***Bruce Almighty***

[42] Carol Kent, *A New Kind of Normal,* (Nashville, TN: Thomas Nelson, 2007), 179

[43] Rob Bell, *Calling All Peacemakers,* Podcast: 12/3 - 12/16/06

[44] Brennan Manning, *Ruthless Trust,* (San Francisco, CA: Harper Collins, 2000), 3 & 4

[45] Les Carter, *Enough About You, Let's Talk About Me,* (San Francisco, CA: Jossey-Bass, 2005), 41

[46] Erwin McManus, *Uprising of the Soul,* (Nashville, TN: Thomas Nelson, 2003), 19

[47] Robert Morgan, *Rules of the Red Sea,* (Nashville, TN: Thomas Nelson, 2001).25 & 26

[48] 47 David Legge, *The Sermon on the Mount - Part 8 - The Subject of Divorce,* 2001, www.preachtheword.com/sermon/sotmo08.shtml

[49] B.A. Robinson, Ontario Consultants on ReligiousTolerance, September 22, 2005, www.religioustolerance.org/div-ok4.htm

CHAPTER 10

[50] Nina W. Brown, *Children of the Self-Absorbed,* (Oakland, CA: New Harbinger Publications, 2001), 16

[51] Peter Jacson, Fran Walsh, J.R.R. Tolken, Philippa Boyen, *Lord of the Rings: The Return of the King*

[52] Cynthia Zayn & Kevin Dibble, *Narcissistic Lovers,* (Far Hills, NJ: New Horizon Press, 2007), 86

[53] Chris Weitz, Paul Weitz, Nick Hornby, Peter Hedge, *About A Boy*

[54] Cynthia Zayn & Kevin Dibble, *Narcissistic Lovers,* (Far Hills, NJ: New Horizon Press, 2007),67

[55] Cynthia Zayn & Kevin Dibble, *Narcissistic Lovers,* (Far Hills, NJ: New Horizon Press, 2007), 91

[56] Erwin McManus, *Uprising of the Soul,* (Nashville, TN: Thomas Nelson, 2003), 144 & 145

[57] Cynthia Zayn & Kevin Dibble, *Narcissistic Lovers,* (Far Hills, NJ: New Horizon Press, 2007), 100

Made in the USA
San Bernardino, CA
10 January 2017